GEORGE ADAMSKI

Flying Saucers and a United World

Three Talks, Detroit 1955

With an introduction and annotations by Gerard Aartsen

Flying Saucers and a United World.
Three Talks, Detroit 1955

Introduced and annotated by Gerard Aartsen.

First published November 2024.

All rights reserved. No part of this book may be reproduced by any means or in any form whatsoever without written permission from the copyright holder(s), except for brief quotations in book reviews.

ISBN-13/EAN-13: 978-90-830336-6-2.

This compilation © BGA Publications, Amsterdam, the Netherlands.

DISCLAIMER: The terms 'Man' and 'Brother' are used in this volume solely in the generic sense of 'humankind' and 'fellow human beings', respectively, without any gender-specific prejudice or preference.

Typeset in Sans Source and Cambria.

Cover design: Meryl Tihanyi.

"Cosmic purposivism may point the way to a new optimism in human potential, based on a humble and open exploration of an unfolding purpose we don't yet fully understand."

Philip Goff
Why? The Purpose of the Universe (2023)

"We should be concerned with much more than merely the dramatic idea of flying through space in manmade craft . . . the coming of these craft establishes a substantiation for man's eventual destiny, which up to now has been but a hope."

George Adamski
A Challenge to Spiritual Leaders (1955)

George Adamski (1891-1965)

Contents

Introduction:
   'The choice lies with Man himself'   1

A Challenge to Spiritual Leaders   21

In My Father's House Are Many Mansions   25

Saucers and Religion   45

The World of Tomorrow   79

Appendices
   I. Saucers! Simple As A.B.C.   113
   II. The physical reality of the visitors from space   123
   III. The Cross over Rome, November 1954   129

Further reading   130

Advertisement for *Inside the Space Ships*
(Abelard-Schuman, 1955)

INTRODUCTION
'The choice lies with Man himself'

After his initial contact with visitors from space in the California desert in November 1952, George Adamski was contacted again several times between February 18, 1953 and April 24, 1955. On a number of these occasions he was invited to board a so-called scout ship, popularly known at the time as a 'flying saucer', and was invited onto a mothership twice.

In September 1955 Adamski went on a lecture tour of the northeastern United States to promote *Inside the Space Ships* in which he details these experiences. While in Detroit, where he gave three lectures, a press conference, as well as media interviews, he challenged the spiritual leaders of his time to share with their followers what they knew about extraterrestrial visitors. Adamski thought that might force the hand of governments who, he said, were withholding information from the public to avoid widespread panic.

Adamski frequently emphasized that the space visitors had a predominantly scientific interest in our planet as they had noticed a beginning shift of the magnetic poles, which might have implications for the rest of the solar system. He also contended that their presence, if publicly acknowledged and accepted, would have profound consequences for life on Earth due to the technological developments that could ensue from open contact, especially in the field of space exploration and how that would boost the economy of a united world.

After newspapers had reported that president Dwight D. Eisenhower, while on an unexpected vacation trip to Palm Springs, California, made an unscheduled disappearance from the Smoke Tree Ranch resort on February 20-21, 1954 there have been persistent rumours that he went to Edwards Air Force Base (a.k.a. Muroc Air Force Base) to meet with visitors from space.[1] The more

---
1   William H. Moore, 'Did President Eisenhower Meet With Aliens in 1954?'. *Hollywood Gazette*, March 29, 1989; and Grant Cameron, 'Eisenhower and the Aliens'. 1 August 2015. See: <whitehouseufo.blogspot.com/2015/08/

fanciful speculations have it that Eisenhower signed a 'treaty' with a group of extraterrestrials that allowed them to abduct a number of citizens in exchange for ET technology.

Researcher Grant Cameron points out that signing a treaty with obviously technologically advanced extraterrestrials would not make much sense, because if they were to violate it, "what would the government do? Take them to court?" Rather, it seems the president had been asked to meet the ETs because they were gravely concerned about the dangers of nuclear weapons and testing — not only for the potential of annihilating ourselves, but also for the threat that the unbridled use of nuclear fission technology in terrestrial conflicts poses to the integrity of the solar system. This they already pointed out in George Adamski's first meeting of November 1952.[2]

This interpretation of the events surrounding Eisenhower's sudden absence finds corroboration in the account of an anonymous participant in the Italian Amicizia, or Friendship Case of contact with extraterrestrials: "... at the end of the '40s, the extraterrestrials offered their collaboration to the head of the USA Administration. In exchange, they asked that the nuclear weaponry program be given up. But their offer and request were rejected ... Following the American politico-military refusal, the space people undertook the strategy consisting in confidential contacts with small groups of terrestrials ... "[3]

This claim in turn was confirmed by a US Air Force test pilot who was one of six people present after three saucer-shaped craft and two cigar-shaped craft landed at Edwards AFB and Eisenhower had been asked to come over from a golf game at nearby Palm Springs to meet the visitors. They spoke English and told the president they wanted to start an education program to increase humanity's awareness of their presence on Earth.[4]

Grant Cameron documents that "only days after the rumored

---

    eisenhower-and-aliens.html>.

2   Len Welch, 'Flying Saucer 'Passenger' Declares A-Bomb Blasts Reason for Visits'. *The Phoenix Gazette*, 24 November 1952.

3   Nikola Duper (2008), 'The story of "Friendship"', [PDF], p.2. Source: <www.scribd.com/document/24686815/Friendship-by-Nikola-Duper>.

4   John Picton, 'Eisenhower Was Visited By UFO, British Lord Claims'. *Sunday Star*, October 24, 1982.

meeting between Eisenhower and the aliens, the American government experienced the worst radiological weapon disaster in history", with the worldwide fallout causing Indian prime minister Jawaharlal Nehru to call for an international moratorium on nuclear tests.

In keeping with the secret nature of the encounter, no official documents have been traced that confirm Eisenhower's meeting with space visitors. However, in May 2010, a citizen blogger was surprised to be told about a brief to president Eisenhower in a conversation with former New Hampshire state legislator Henry W. McElroy Jr:

> After I asked Rep. McElroy about his viewpoint concerning life in other galaxies, which was considerably off-topic for the conversation we were having, he paused slightly. His head turned sideways, and he proceeded to make a statement that spurred my interest immediately.
>
> "Of course, there's life in other galaxies," he said. "I saw that brief to Eisenhower, when I was in office."
>
> "Excuse me?" I said. "What brief are you talking about?"
>
> "The brief. To Eisenhower. Telling him that they wanted to have a meeting with him," he said.
>
> "Who wanted to have a meeting with him?" I said, not really understanding where this conversation was going.
>
> "Extraterrestrials," he said. "They were here. During the fifties. I saw the brief to Eisenhower, telling him that they wanted to meet with him."

In order to share this with the world at large it was decided that Mr. McElroy record a public address, in which he stated: "The document I saw was an official brief to President Eisenhower. To the best of my memory this brief was pervaded with a sense of hope, and it informed President Eisenhower of the continued presence of extraterrestrial beings here in the United States of America. The brief seemed to indicate that a meeting between the President and some of these visitors could be arranged as appropriate, if desired."[5]

In his talk of September 19, 1955 George Adamski suggests he knows about Eisenhower's meeting when he says: "If President Eisenhower told you the truth — which he has — if he ran for re-election next year he'd be beaten..." (Pages 30 and 53)

According to several sources Adamski held a US Government ordnance card for access to certain restricted areas, as well as a passport bearing special privileges.[6] And in private correspondence he mentions several high ranking military or intelligence people visiting him at Palomar Gardens, while other accounts attest to his private meetings with president Kennedy in 1962 regarding the Cuba crisis[7], and with Pope John XXIII in 1963[8], both with messages from his space contacts. His residence on the slopes of Palomar Mountain was within driving distance of both Palm Springs and Edwards AFB, so if he did attend the meeting between Eisenhower and the extraterrestrials, this could have been the occasion when he was introduced to the highest echelons of government as the primary ambassador for the space visitors, and would explain how he came by the documents granting him the special access privileges.

But, as he told his audience on September 20, 1955, "I don't betray a trust once it is placed in me." (Page 107) His later Swiss associate Lou Zinsstag revealed after his death: "He once told me when we were alone that he was entrusted with many secrets from both sides of the fence (this was his expression), from the US government as well as from the [Space] Brothers, and this because he never once broke a vow of silence, he would rather play the fool when asked."[9]

---

5 Brief To Eisenhower blog (archived). See: <web.archive.org/web/20100618075637/http://brieftoeisenhower.wordpress.com/>; 'Former Legislator Makes Statement on Un-Released Eisenhower Brief'. See also: <www.youtube.com/watch?v=kFqzx6SUY6c>.

6 Timothy Good (1998), *Alien Base – Earth's Encounters with Extraterrestrials*, pp.138-140.

7 Zinsstag, 'On George Adamski', *UFO Contact* Vol.3, No.5, September 1967, p.137.

8 Zinsstag, 'Adamski in Rome', *Flying Saucer Review*, Vol.11, No.6, November-December 1965, pp.22-23.

9 Lou Zinsstag, 'On George Adamski', op cit.

As history has shown, Eisenhower refrained from publicly acknowledging the extraterrestrial presence and their intentions, while the successive governmental committees that were purportedly set up to investigate the many reports of unidentified flying objects were effectively covering up whatever could be seen as confirmation of the reality of the visitors. On several occasions George Adamski stated that all the (major?) governments of the world had been contacted by the visitors. What is more, in a talk on July 21, 1963 he said that president Eisenhower "knew who it was when he [Eisenhower] associated with a man from Saturn".[10]

With the USA coming out of World War 2 as one of the two remaining superpowers, the other of course being the impenetrable Soviet Union, and the US bankrolling the reconstruction of countries that had been ravaged by war, as well as the defence against the perceived threat of Communism, no government would risk provoking America's displeasure. For these reasons Adamski said, "The governments of the world have gone as far as they can go, so don't look for anything greater from them." (Page 54)

In a letter to a correspondent Adamski delves into the reasons for the government's reluctance to inform the public: "As for Tesla, Hendershot, Roberts and the others you mentioned, I have often discussed them[11], their efforts and the results, and am in full agreement with your statement, 'This may be the secret behind all the hush-hush and persecution.' Actually the interplanetary visitations are a minor affair, but the propulsion of these craft is of major importance. That is why all attempts [at disclosure] up to the present day have been fought, and people persecuted and jailed. Things have not changed much! In fact, today they are intensified, for these powers are greater than ever."[12]

About his recent lecture tour of the eastern USA he recounts: "While in New York I met a very reliable man who knows a little about this. He said, 'Look George, just think of the chaos in the world

---

10 F.B. [Alfred Bailey?], 'Notes from Adamski Lectures (1963-1965)', p.3.

11 See also page 83.

12 Note that Adamski's observations in this regard predate Dr Steven Greer's statements in the 2023 documentary *The Lost Century – And How to Reclaim It* by almost seven decades.

if such a machine once becomes recognized by the masses. Can you not see doors closing in banks everywhere, and money becoming worthless — at least for a while? The bottom of the world would fall out, for the world is founded on a pillar of gold and the manipulation of its value. No, this cannot be allowed to happen, and the powers that be will do anything and everything to prevent it from happening, even to the point of wars. They will go so far as to take a chance on self-annihilation to preserve the foundation. Yet with hopes that they may survive when others are gone.' "[13]

In an earlier letter to the same correspondent Adamski writes: "Judging from my mail, Catholics, Protestants, Jews, Orientals, all religions and people from all walks of life are interested in and supporting the space visitations from the physical, mechanical point of view, while few of them indeed would be interested if it were thrown in the mysterious. And when the people of the world begin thinking in accord on such a subject, the foundations of the money changers begins to weaken. When people's eyes are turned upward, searching the skies for friendly space visitors, even in a small degree among men here, it becomes more difficult to fill their minds with hatred for their fellowmen wherein war finds a fertile field. And youthful minds filled with challenging thoughts of space travel are not so easily diverted toward the rather questionable honor awaiting in bloody battlefields. Is this what the financiers see and fear? I think it is!"[14]

Interestingly, though, it was the deeply spiritual message that his more advanced contacts from space — Space Brothers, as he called them — asked him to share with the world, that resonated most strongly with a public eager to read about his experiences in *Inside the Space Ships*. When this was published in 1955, George Adamski's account of how he met an extraterrestrial visitor in the California Desert had already reached people in all corners of the world. *Flying Saucers Have Landed* (1953), which detailed the historic events of November 1952, had been published in nine different languages already, including Japanese and Hebrew.

---

[13] Adamski, Letter to Gray Barker, June 8, 1955. Reproduced in Barker (1980), *The Adamski Documents*, Part 1.

[14] Adamski, Letter to Gray Barker, March 11, 1955. Reproduced in Barker (1980), op cit.

In *Inside the Space Ships* Adamski followed up with the even more astonishing account of his subsequent meetings with visitors from space, when he was invited on board their craft on multiple occasions and even taken on trips into space. But more than his fascinating descriptions of how these meetings took place, the technical details of the ships and their propulsion, and the sensation of travelling in space, what stood out in this book was the information about his hosts' approach to life. Their morals and ethics seemed to have evolved in step with their technological advances — or perhaps it would be better to say that the latter had been made possible by the fact that they *live* according to their professed values.

In his challenge to the spiritual leaders of his time Adamski argues that "the dramatic idea of flying through space in manmade craft" is only a minor concern. "Once this is realized, the coming of these craft establishes a substantiation for man's eventual destiny" because "it is bound to broaden Earthman's consciousness into a more Cosmic conception, lifting him far above his present confining ignorance". (Page 21) And if church leaders would educate their followers the anticipated panic could be avoided: "Since the Church has taken on the responsibility of bringing to man an understanding of his relationship to his Creator, it would seem to be the Church's duty to proclaim the reality of these interplanetary visitations and the truth that surrounds them. This then would guarantee a reverent instead of hostile attitude on the part of all peoples." (Page 22)

Indeed, it seems the visitors had already begun to 'reintroduce' themselves to church leaders when a formation of UFOs formed an Andrew's Cross over the Vatican in November 1954 (page 129). In a letter to Italian consul Alberto Perego, George Adamski explained: "The reason for the numerous manoeuvres over Rome, such as those you witnessed on 6 November 1954, must be sought in the intention of raising people's interest, given that Rome is the seat of the Christian religion. These impressions on the masses will affect the Holy See which will end up proclaiming the existence of these craft. This will lead the world to accept the friendly attitude of these interplanetary visitors. And no longer to consider it hostile and fearful, as it has generally been presented. (. . .) Since the Cross is the symbol of the Christian religion, the 'cross' formation over Rome was intended to demonstrate that these visitors (...) recognize the universal spirit of Christ and they want the inhabitants of the Earth to understand that they behave according to his commandment: to be brothers."[15]

Obviously we don't know if it was at the suggestion from his space contacts or his own idea to try and get the religious leaders to encourage their flocks to demand disclosure. And although the fact that Earth is a regular destination for visitors from space is a common notion in all or most major religions, since the USA and the West were the centre of gravity of world power and cultural dominance after WW2, Adamski's challenge was aimed primarily at the leaders of the Christian faith.

Either way, Adamski had reason to believe there was a chance his words would fall on receptive ears. According to a former member of the Vatican intelligence service SIV, John's predecessor Pius XII had already been contacted by the space people twice in the Vatican gardens at the Pontifical Academy of Sciences.[16] And in a letter to *Flying Saucer Review* Lou Zinsstag reminisced: "I had accompanied George to Rome already in 1959 and I still remember his urgent wish to see the Pope, Pius, in a private interview. This aim, however, was not achieved in 1959."[17]

Although unjustly disputed, Adamski did manage to meet privately with John XXIII in May 1963[18] who, according to reports, had himself met with visitors from space at least twice. In 1985 the Pope's private secretary Loris Capovilla related the meeting that took place in the gardens at the papal summer residence Castel Gandolfo one evening in July 1961. As monsignor Capovilla accompanied the Pope on a stroll through the gardens they noticed

---

15 Adamski, Letter to Alberto Perego, April 20, 1956. Retranslated from the Italian in Perego (1963), *L'aviazione di altri pianeti opera tra noi: rapporto agli italiani: 1943-1963*, pp.540-41.

16 Cristoforo Barbato, 'Intervista al Gesuita, Rome 2001'. See: <www.usac.it/articoli/CristoforoBarbato/intervista_al_gesuita/Intervista_al_Gesuita.html>.

17 Lou Zinsstag, 'Adamski in Rome', op cit, p.22. Note: Her reference to Pius XII must have been due to a memory lapse, since John XXIII succeeded Pius upon the latter's demise in 1958.

18 For the correct chronology and circumstances of events surrounding Adamski's meeting with John XXIII, see Aartsen (2019), *George Adamski – The facts in context*, 'Vatican Visit': <www.the-adamski-case.nl/his-mission/vatican-visit/>.

an unusual craft in the air: "It was oval and had blue and amber flashing lights. The craft seemed to fly over our heads for a few minutes and then landed on the grass at the south end of the garden. A strange being came out of the craft. He looked human, except that he was surrounded by a golden light. The Pope and I knelt down. We didn't know what we were witnessing. But we knew that it was not from this world, so it must have been a celestial event. The Holy Father stood up and walked towards the being. From their gesturing it seemed they spoke intensely for about 15-20 minutes. They did not call me, so I remained where I was and could not hear what they were discussing. Then the being turned around and walked towards the craft which left right away. The Pontiff came towards me and said: 'The sons of God are everywhere. Sometimes we have difficulties in recognizing our own brothers'."

Remarkably, rather than being denied or discounted by the Vatican, this papal experience was later recounted by Costa Rican bishop Higinio Alas Gómes in talks and interviews.[19] Also, Fr. Segundo B. Reyna, a Jesuit priest who was the Director of the Adhara Astronomical Observatory in Buenos Aires, Argentina and himself an eyewitness to various UFO sightings, freely shared the story of Adamski's private audience with Pope John XXIII. Perhaps the most telling evidence that Adamski actually did meet the Pope is the fact that he was the first to mention the extraterrestrial visits to the Vatican in a talk on September 8, 1963 when he stated that two landings of space craft had taken place during John XXIII's papacy.[20] How would he know this, unless the Pope told him about it?

In a talk on August 11, 1963 Adamski revealed that Pope John had a meeting with Soviet leader Nikita Krushchev's son-in-law where he passed on important information regarding the people from space. He wanted to see president Kennedy too, to share the same information with him, so that anything coming from the Kremlin could not be dismissed as propaganda. "Kennedy and Krushchev both have the information and the first step to peace was the recent

---

19 'Juan XXIII Contactado por Extraterrestres: Higinio Alas'. See: <www.youtube.com/watch?v=PWouSgRAw6I&t=553s>
20 F.B., 'Notes from Adamski Lectures', op cit, p.12.

signing of the new [nuclear] test ban treaty."[21] Various reports indicate that Adamski met with Kennedy several times, and that he acted as a liaison between the extraterrestrials and the president.[22]

For the promotion of his new book George Adamski travelled to the northeastern United States in June and September 1955 on a publicity tour comprising many lectures and media interviews. The press conference and talks in Detroit were organised by Laura Mundo Marxer. A local TV personality, Mrs Marxer first learned of Adamski's experiences when a friend gave her a copy of *Flying Saucers Have Landed*. In April 1954 Adamski spoke to over 4,500 people at the Detroit Masonic Hall, where she stood on the platform with him and helped field questions from the audience. She soon founded the Study Group of Interplanetary Relations, and later the Flying Saucer Information Center that served the many flying saucer groups in greater Detroit and Michigan. Over time, she claimed her own experiences with the space visitors, who she said "sent a beam of neutronic energy of the Father Frequency to my brain", drawing a group of followers through her 'understandings' that followed, causing Adamski to keep a distance from her. Although she no longer supported Adamski in the 1960s, she continued to write about flying saucers and her own 'understandings'.[23]

In the talks following his challenge to the religious leaders Adamski employs very literal interpretations of Biblical texts, although not in the fundamentalist sense of claiming the Bible to be the literal word of God. Rather, he equates Heaven with Cosmos and makes similar comparisons based on literal representations of Biblical concepts and stories. Perhaps he was giving the clergy cues for informing their flocks in terms that people would understand or be willing to accept.

Yet, despite the seemingly simplistic explanations for Biblical statements, and although some of his expectations for the future now seem outdated or have proven premature by subsequent world

---

21 Ibidem, p.7.
22 Good (2013), *Earth. An Alien Enterprise*, pp.382-385.
23 Wikitree, 'Laura Charlotte (Mundo) Marxer'. See: <www.wikitree.com/wiki/Mundo-10>.

events, several other notions show his remarkable foresight, for instance regarding the various global crises that we are witnessing today, as well as the need for global unity to solve them.

While the threat of annihilation through nuclear conflict was psychologically tangible from the end of WW2 until it gradually receded into the background at the time of détente beginning in 1969, in recent years it has reared its ugly head again. What progress was made in terms of international cooperation has been steadily undone with the unleashing of neoliberal market forces since the 1980s and the covert meddling in smaller countries' domestic affairs for access to raw materials or markets. The subsequent commodification and competition have increased global tensions which in turn, according to a 2024 report, caused a record 13 per cent rise in global spending on nuclear weapons.[24]

Adamski doesn't mince his words when he says, "If we take the road we've been taking, then destruction is awaiting us!" (Page 48) This was echoed in Secretary General Antonio Guterres's warning in 2022: "The idea that any country could fight and win a nuclear war is deranged. Any use of a nuclear weapon would incite a humanitarian Armageddon. We need to step back."[25] As Adamski said, "The choice lies with Man himself." (Page 23)

In *The Adamski Book of UFO/UAP Disclosure* I documented how Adamski foresaw the rise of the military-industrial complex six years before president Eisenhower warned against it in his farewell speech: "Acceptance of the reality of Interplanetary Visitors could and would have far-reaching effects upon the present-day economic system on Earth. Everybody would be affected in some ways, but the few would be affected in a far greater degree. I believe they see this and are fighting it with everything they have . . ."[26]

As a result of the neocolonial economic diktats of the richest countries and megacorporations that have robbed many people

---

24 Dan Sabbagh, 'Global spending on nuclear weapons up 13% in record rise'. *The Guardian*, June 17, 2024.

25 'UN Chief calls for an end to 'nuclear blackmail' and risk of 'humanitarian Armageddon'. *UN News*, September 26, 2022. See: <news.un.org/en/story/2022/09/1127961>.

26 Adamski, Letter to Gray Barker, March 11, 1955, op cit.

in developing countries of their livelihoods and denied millions a decent income for themselves and their families, millions of people are now migrating, legally or illegally, to places where they expect to find at least some opportunity to earn a living. This has created a migration crisis that affects almost every Western country and has given rise to increasing support for short-sighted selfish border protection policies that are proving ineffective in keeping people from seeking paid labour and prospects for the future of their children. This, too, Adamski saw coming when he said in reference to the occupation of Indochina: ". . . in those days the yellow races, the colored races all over the world will rise and demand the rights that white men have enjoyed through all these ages." (Pages 27 and 79) This comment could equally be seen as foretelling the rise of the civil rights movement in the US.

In comments about pollution and clean sources of energy, we see how his concerns foreshadow the climate crises now engulfing the world as a result of humanity's inaction in response to the warnings of scientists about transgressing Earth's natural boundaries in terms of pollution and the exploitation of minerals and other natural resources: " . . . we find a great disturbance in the world of the human mind [and] Mother Earth, herself, gets a little shaky . . . Just how far she's going to go with it is anybody's guess . . . But we do know that there's something going on in this world and we do know that this year we had quite a number of bad conditions produced by nature. Millions of dollars lost, disasters caused by hurricanes; hot weather . . . were it was not known before." (Page 84)

Most significant, perhaps — and most ignored, are Adamski's repeated references to this time in history, this transitional period between two cosmic cycles:

> "The main thing is not a question of saucers, my experiences or anybody else's. The main thing is what is really transpiring in this world." (Page 25)

> The Bible "tells us that after 2000 years — which they called a dispensation — a new dispensation would enter. That the old would pass away and the new would come." (Page 38)

"...when these things will be happening — like 'signs in the sky and war and rumors of war' — we will have come to an end of a cycle, or as some people call it, a 'dispensation'." (Page 79)

"It's not only our own Earth but the whole system that is going through a change which is a cycle that is coming to an end and another will take its place." (Page 86)

"There is something transpiring in this world that we never dreamed would take place in our time, but it is taking place — the tendency toward a United World." (Page 87)

In these statements we find the underlying reason for the expanded extraterrestrial presence on Earth at this juncture in history — to help humanity get through this time of transition with as little self-harm as possible. We already have the United Nations Organisation, the only hope the world has for a future where international conflicts can be resolved justly and peacefully if it is allowed to take up its rightful role as the parliament of nations in the United World that Adamski foresees here. But in order to fulfil that role, the UN Security Council will need to be abolished, where the major powers frustrate any effort at international cooperation that gets in the way of their own geopolitical or short-term interests.

The notion of Earth moving out of one cosmic cycle and into a new cycle has long been dismissed as 'unscientific' or just a fantasy, because the cosmic constellations that comprise the Zodiac are seen by science as mere random groupings by the ancients, and would be too distant from the Earth to have any noticeable effect on terrestrial life.

However, it is becoming ever clearer that the ancients had a far deeper understanding of astronomy than they have been given credit for. Also, it is now an established fact that our planet is constantly bombarded with cosmic radiation, while Cosmos and even the foundation of its three-dimensional appearance are seen as oceans of energy that our science is only beginning to understand. Quantum science and consciousness research inform us that everything that exists, within or outside our range of vision, is intricately interconnected, which makes the notion that our solar system may be under the cyclic energetic influence of distant cosmic constellations suddenly much less outlandish. A true scientist would take these combined facts as a cue to look into the possible or probable merits of ancient astrological claims — rather than dismissing the entire notion on the basis of generic tabloid horoscope columns.

Without explicitly referring to specific zodiacal constellations, like Pisces or Aquarius, the above statements from the three talks compiled in this volume show that Adamski was well aware of the cosmic energetic causes and effects of consecutive cycles, as the solar system travels through galactic space. From his very first publication, *The Invisible Ocean*, until his very last, the *Science of Life* study course, he shared his indisputable knowledge and experience that we live in a sea of consciousness, and that our individual consciousness is in the process of expanding to the point where the infinite potential of its Source becomes manifest in human form, as demonstrated in the highly evolved civilizations of his space contacts. Human history is rich with individual examples of such manifestations, whether they be the universal genius of great artists, such as for example Leonardo da Vinci or Shakespeare, or human incarnations of the Divine, such as Krishna, Buddha or Christ, who point humanity the way forward at the beginning or end of every cosmic cycle — before their guidance becomes corrupted when followers begin to organise their teachings and theological doctrine sets in.

Careful study of earlier passages from one cycle to the next will show that such Teachers unfailingly emerge at times of transition like the present, and there is no reason why this age would be an exception. All major religions agree in their expectation of the coming or return of a Teacher, whether they await him as the Messiah, the Second Coming of Christ, the fifth Buddha, the tenth incarnation of Vishnu, or the twelfth Mahdi, sometimes known as Muntazar.

In the early 20th century the Theosophical Society, founded by Helena Blavatsky, who was the first to postulate the fundamental nature and evolution of consciousness, started preparing for the coming of the World Teacher for this age.[27] At the end of WW2, the Tibetan Master of Wisdom Djwhal Khul revealed the Teacher's decision to return as soon as possible[28], which it was hoped would be around 1950, but again humanity was drawn into conflict — the Cold War this time. In 1982 Scottish artist and esotericist Benjamin Creme announced that the World Teacher had taken up his place in the modern world, awaiting the time when humanity would be receptive enough for his call for global justice and sharing, as the first steps towards the manifestation on the physical plane of humanity's essential oneness, proclaiming: "When you share, you recognize God in your brother."[29]

In an essay from 1958 Adamski writes that his space contacts showed him this is the way forward: "Our neighbours, I have been told, have long since learnt to solve their problems without resorting to the barbaric practice of war. They have learnt to respect one another as children of the Infinite, and have overcome personal greed by working together and sharing the products of their world so that no one is in want."[30] And in reference to the return of a Teacher amid our failing political and economic structures Adamski once said: "Were Jesus to return and be accepted, it would mean that all of our present systems would be overthrown to make way for His Cosmic Teachings. Are we prepared for this?"[31]

The reader who is willing to consider this scenario will not find it difficult to understand that this is, to use Adamski's words, "what is really transpiring in this world". And this transition to what for most people will be a world based on a wholly new perspective of life and reality is the true significance of this time in human history that has elicited the massive appearance of extraterrestrial craft, beginning with the first detonation of an atom bomb in a global

---

27 Joseph E. Ross (2000), *Krishnamurti: The Taormina Seclusion*, 1912.
28 Alice A. Bailey (1948), *The Reappearance of the Christ*, p.69.
29 Benjamin Creme (ed.; 1981), *Messages from Maitreya the Christ*, Message No.82, September 18, 1979.
30 S.K. Maitra (ed.; 1958), *We Are Not Alone in the Universe*, p.4, as reprinted in Aartsen (2022), *The Adamski Book of UFO/UAP Disclosure – Early evidence and answers now confirmed by science, philosophers, activists and the military*, p.88.
31 Adamski (1958), *Cosmic Science*, Part 5, Question 94.

conflict. As the state of the world in 2024 makes abundantly clear, humanity is indeed, as Adamski puts it, at a crossroads, where we will decide whether to continue into ever increasing competition, conflict and chaos, or go forward in cooperation towards the safe progress of our planetary evolution. Our choice will also decide if we will rejoin the interplanetary brotherhood of our solar system, and finally begin to contribute the unique evolutionary experience of our species to the greater cosmic good.

Is there any scientific evidence to substantiate such unconventional claims? As with much of our present-day scientific assumptions, there is no direct proof, but by triangulating evidence from different disciplines we can arrive at a solid foundation for this perspective.

As I argued elsewhere, religion — any religion, when the essential teaching is stripped of centuries of manmade dogma and doctrine — is fundamentally a signpost or technique to help the people of that time and in that part of the world to reconnect their individual consciousness (the Self, soul, Christ in us, Atman, divine spark, Krishna consciousness, etc.) with the Source of consciousness (God, Brahma, Allah, the Absolute, etc.). It is to this purpose that the original Latin for the word 'religion' — *re ligare*, to reconnect — refers. And if the different faiths would unite in acknowledging the extraterrestrial presence, Adamski says, it "would inevitably lead to further unity in which the hairs of difference in creed and dogma would no longer seem worth splitting." (Page 21-22)

According to scientists, "there is a shift occurring in the way we understand reality, precisely because our current world view is reaching its limits. People are beginning to understand the world and themselves as interconnected, rather than as individual entities bound together only by cause and effect."[32] In recent years post-materialist science has found that the physical sciences can't give a satisfactory explanation for the emergence of consciousness from the chemical processes in the brain, because they only deal with the material side of our three-dimensional existence.[33] Based on

---

32 Sarah Durston and Ton Baggerman (2017), *The Universe, Life and Everything*, p.9. See: <library.oapen.org/handle/20.500.12657/31132>.

33 See e.g. Harald Walach (2019), *Beyond a Materialist World View – Towards an Expanded Science*.

his synthesis of the findings of various scientific disciplines Ervin Laszlo has concluded, "The universe, as we now know, is not a domain of matter moving in passive space and indifferently flowing in time; it is a sea of coherent vibrations."[34] In 1932 George Adamski already asserted a strikingly similar notion in *The Invisible Ocean*: "... I am in the invisible ocean of vibrations or consciousness."[35]

Professor Laszlo's findings further indicate that the "clusters of coordinated vibration" that together make up that sea are 'in-formed' by an underlying intelligence — which it wouldn't be difficult to equate with the religious notion of God or Brahma, or more universally the Infinite, or the Source. And, continues Laszlo, "The closer the clusters [such as the physical life forms] vibrate to the deep dimension [of the cosmos], the more they are in-formed by the intelligence intrinsic to the cosmos."[36]

In his recent book *Why? The Purpose of the Universe* science philosopher Philip Goff explains how incredibly unlikely the existence of the Universe would be without an underlying intelligence which alone can explain the meticulous fine-tuning of all the variables that was necessary to even bring the cosmic particles into existence that we are all made of. He concludes his book, saying: "We can only ignore the evidence of cosmological fine-tuning for so long. And my sense is that the public are ceasing to believe that the mind–body problem is just a scientific problem we are one experiment from solving." Hinting at the paradigm shift that the more discerning observer can see taking place before our very eyes: "A radical change in how we see the universe is on its way."[37] Indeed, says Laszlo, "To integrate, harmonize, and unify all things, and at the same time embrace all things in oneness and love, is the Telos [goal] of all existence."[38]

Here we arrive, based on scientific findings, at a strikingly similar purpose as the essential religious teachings — to reconnect

---

34 Ervin Laszlo (2017), *The Intelligence of the Cosmos. New Answers from the Frontiers of Science*, p.46.
35 Adamski (1932), *The Invisible Ocean*, pp.10-11.
36 Laszlo (2016), *What Is Reality? The New Map of Cosmos and Consciousness*, p.15.
37 Philip Goff (2023), *Why? The Purpose of the Universe*, p.150.
38 Laszlo (2017), op cit. p.47.

with the source of life and consciousness. Jesus of Nazareth said, "I (the individual consciousness) and the Father (the cosmic Source) are One"; Indian philosophy says, "I am That", and the Greek Oracle of Delphi told us, "Man, know thyself and ye will know all things". Astronomer Carl Sagan realized we are inevitably searching for that oneness when he said: "We are a way for the cosmos to know itself." And let us not forget, throughout his teachings, from long before his personal contacts started as well as in the messages from the space visitors, George Adamski's philosophy asserts the exact same notion: "I believe this whole phenomenon has reached a point where it should be recognized as a fulfillment of long cherished dreams and hopes, whereby Man once again will understand his relationship to the Cosmos itself." (Page 22)

At the moment though, says Goff, "we are living through a scary, uncertain era. Nothing has filled the vacuum left by the decline of traditional religions. And whilst the 2008 global meltdown gave the lie to the delusion that Wild West capitalism will provide peace and prosperity for all, no political philosophy has come along to replace neo-liberalism. (. . .) Times of big change can be frightening, but they are also pregnant with opportunities for renewal. We have every reason to feel optimistic about the future."

It is this optimism that these talks by George Adamski exude. It is this positive realism that informed his understanding of the conscious purpose towards greater unity underlying cosmic conditions and world developments that are only now being discovered and considered by trailblazing scientists like Philip Goff, Ervin Laszlo, Harald Walach and many others.

Most 'serious' UFO researchers dismiss Adamski's account and views as 'evangelical' or derided them as a 'UFO religion'. Now science is catching up with him. Who will be next?

Disclosure activists?
Policy makers?
You?

Gerard Aartsen
October 2024

Three Talks
and a Challenge

Editor's notes:
The talks compiled in this volume were recorded on audio tape and transcripts were made available by the Interplanetary Foundation of Detroit, Michigan to those interested. The transcript of the first talk was earlier published in a private, limited edition as 'Many Mansions' in 1974 and 1983.

For the purpose of this compilation all transcripts were retyped, with spelling made consistent and obvious typing errors corrected. Any typing or spelling errors in this compilation are the current editor's. Footnotes provide historical context were references are made to people, events, publications or organisations that present-day readers may not be familiar with.

These talks were given on consecutive days in September 1955 and inevitably there is some overlap in the subjects covered. Footnotes with cross references will refer the reader to remarks on the same subject in the other talks, for a fuller picture of Adamski's thoughts on that subject.

At a press conference with the ministers of Detroit in September 1955, George Adamski issued this challenge to religious leaders and shared some of his experiences with space visitors, allying these with Biblical history in his subsequent talk (p.25 ff). A question and answer period followed the lecture and is given here in its entirety.

A Challenge to Spiritual Leaders

by George Adamski

I am not looking to any governmental or military group, regardless of nation, to bring out the truth of the Space Visitors. If they did, they too would be questioned by the majority of the people and the whole thing would remain as controversial as it is today. It would be placed or left (as at present) subject to a hostile interpretation in the minds of many.

There is but one answer to a problem which is far from a small one, for this enigma of interplanetary visitations is of a universal aspect, dealing as it does with universal principles. We should be concerned with much more than merely the dramatic idea of flying through space in manmade craft. That is a very minute part of the whole. Once this is realized, the coming of these craft establishes a substantiation for man's eventual destiny, which up to now has been but a hope. Not only that, but it is bound to broaden Earthman's consciousness into a more Cosmic conception, lifting him far above his present confining ignorance. In challenging him to think in terms of Cosmos and his relation thereto, he will forget the puny differences which have brought him to grief on this Earth through the ages.

The reality of these ships from other planets *belongs in the realm of the Cosmos*. Therefore, those who could best bring forth the truth to the whole of mankind and establish friendly relations between the visitors and ourselves would be *the great religions of the world*, united in at least this one purpose. Such union would inevitably lead to further unity in which the hairs of difference in creed and dogma would no longer seem worth splitting. I believe this whole phenomenon has reached a point where it should be recognized as a fulfillment of long cherished dreams and hopes, whereby Man once again will understand his relationship to the Cosmos itself.

Since the Church has taken on the responsibility of bringing to man an understanding of his relationship to his Creator, it would seem to be the Church's duty to proclaim the reality of these interplanetary visitations and the truth that surrounds them. This then would guarantee a reverent instead of hostile attitude on the part of all peoples. In achieving this, the Church would then establish an understanding state of mind whereby definite visitation would follow, permitting our more evolved Brothers to give us more useful information of the Universe about which we as yet know so little. The Space Brothers could then be welcomed in our homes and cities as friends and teachers.

Outstanding evidence in the teachings of all great religions to substantiate this possibility can be found. For example, one of the greatest religions, the Catholic, acknowledges that a human body born in this world *can* be taken elsewhere in earthly form to a place which they call Heaven. This is what is described in the Resurrection of Jesus and, more recently, in their acknowledgment that the Virgin Mary herself left in this manner. Then there was Elijah who was carried off in a "fiery chariot", and many other similar accounts.

The Lord's Prayer itself is an acknowledgement of a world or place called *Heaven*. "Thy Will be done on Earth as it is in Heaven." If the Father's Will can be done on Earth as it is in Heaven, it is an admission that the Earth can become better, or like Heaven. Also, an admission that bodies *can* be taken from this world in bodily form to some Nirvana in the skies. By the same token, it constitutes an acknowledgment that men could in bodily form come from there to here.

Since the Lord's Prayer asks that it be done Earth as it is in Heaven, how could this be accomplished unless the heavenly-type being, man or woman, comes to Earth from a happier abode and teaches us their way, that we might be enlightened sufficiently to establish our own heaven on Earth, as they *have done* on their worlds?

All of this points the finger to the great religions, by whatever name they are known, as the responsible source to bring this Truth to mankind. Did not Jesus himself say, "In my Father's house are many mansions?"

If the great Churches or religions fail their flocks in this case, then they must shoulder the guilt for whatever may happen to mankind on Earth from here on. We are at the final crossroads. One of two things can happen. With the aid of these Visitors we can go on to become the greatest and *only enduring* civilization this world has ever known — enduring because *the peoples of the world will be united* — or we can completely annihilate one another through atomic conflict, as is well known by all major scientists.

Thus, the necessity for this proclamation of Truth regarding the *reality* of our interplanetary Brothers coming our way is far more serious than the average person can guess. Receptive minds and widespread coverage are *musts* in order that people throughout the world may understand what is at stake. Prophecy, as it has been written, will be fulfilled one way or the other; either the Kingdom of Heaven *will* be established on this Earth — or complete annihilation of Earth's inhabitants will be the inevitable result. The choice lies with Man himself. *But the initial responsibility rests on the shoulders of the spiritual leaders throughout the world.*

George Adamski with TV host Steve Allen (left)

"I was on Steve Allen's television show when I was in New York recently and I was told, 'Don't let anyone put words in your mouth. We've been told to play this whole thing down.'"
(Pages 28 and 46-47.)

In My Father's House Are Many Mansions

Talk by George Adamski

Well, friends, as much as I do not like this kind of job I have to do it. But I have made the trip; my book is out and the publishing house wants it to be known by my appearance here and there. I didn't expect to come out at this time. I intended to be in Mexico City by now. Instead, I'll have to make this trip and go to Mexico City as soon as I return to California.

The main thing is NOT a question of saucers, my experiences or anybody else's. The main thing is WHAT IS REALLY TRANSPIRING IN THIS WORLD. THAT is more important than any individual or any phenomenon that is taking place at this moment. We do know what we have taught — and this is where the religious question comes up. The latest issue of *Time* magazine (Sept. 19 issue) has an article, 'Space Theology'.[1] Probably you have seen it. Very good. They seem to be lining up very well because the movement is worldwide. You'll be hearing more of it as time goes on. The saucer, it might be said, has done its job and done it well. Even if they never appeared again, we'll never live the same. That's one sure thing.

All eyes have, through skeptical methods or otherwise, been focused on space. Especially since Eisenhower and the other three Powers that met at Geneva made a simultaneous announcement of a satellite going out into space.[2]

The odd part is, I have mentioned that there is air beyond our own atmosphere. At that time they told us there was only a vacuum. Yet, when they made this announcement they said the satellite would wear itself out due to the friction that it will encounter because of the *air being there* which is lighter than our own. This

---

1 See: <time.com/archive/6802838/religion-space-theology/>.
2 In preparation for the International Geophysical Year (IGY) of 1957-58, in July 1955 the US announced plans to launch its first satellites, with France, Great Britain and the USSR following suit. See also page 51.

confirms what I have said — a statement many people laughed at. But things will work themselves out in the end and will bring out the truth. The shadows will fall away and the light will shine, in other words.[3]

But, we have been taught through the ages that a great Messiah, known as Jesus Christ to the world, was born in a manger, of flesh no different than that of yours and mine. We have been told that He, too, had taken that particular body out of this world into the sky, called Heaven. For everything of so-called Heaven is always placed in the sky. A couple of years ago the Catholic Church announced the same thing in honoring the Virgin Mary on the same grounds.

We also find that the great Teacher has taught us: "In My Father's house are many mansions. I go to prepare a place for you that you may also be there." He also called this world a mansion, no different from what He told you He was preparing somewhere else up in the sky. Yet He was asked where the Kingdom of Heaven was and the answer came from Him, "The Kingdom of Heaven is *within you.*" In other words, you may live in a Heaven right now but if you have not learned how to *live* in Heaven you wouldn't know you are in Heaven — anymore than you could be taken into a palace for the first time and know how to live there until you have learned how.[4] So, that could have meant that very well.

Then we are told about Elijah, Enoch and many others. There are about 350 cases in Biblical history of (landings, or contacts with) spacecraft, as we call them today, known under different names at different periods that they have appeared. In each case in this Biblical history we find an acknowledgement that if a man's human body, as we know it on this Earth today, had a way of leaving here — it could go somewhere else and continue to live.[5]

---

3 See e.g. Gerard Aartsen (2022), *The Adamski Book of UFO/UAP Disclosure – Early evidence and answers now confirmed by science, philosophers, activists and the military.*

4 This echoes what Adamski said in his final letter to his student Emma Martinelli, dated May 8, 1952. See Aartsen (ed.; 2022), *George Adamski – Letters to Emma Martinelli,* p.97.

5 Being at pains to emphasize that his contacts were with real beings amid

We find in The Lord's Prayer, "Thy Will be done on Earth as it is in Heaven." How in the world are you and I going to do anything on Earth as it is in Heaven unless someone comes this way and tells us what's to be done. It also tells us something like this: that the Son of Man will be coming from Heaven to Earth — and Heaven has always meant in reference to the sky. To see what time we're living in, it states that in those days the yellow races, the colored races all over the world will rise and demand the rights that white men have enjoyed through all these ages — and where's your trouble in Asia?[6] What more evidence do we want than what is transpiring in this world at the present time? All these teachings up to now — are the leaders of the great religions institutions going to back down on it now and say, "We were just teaching you a little fairy story all this time"? Or will they acknowledge it? And they almost have to — for let me show you something that is happening.

I get thousands of letters, *Collier's* magazine[7] has interviewed me several times. They've taken some of my letters and are going to put them into an article which will come out sometime this fall. We find here, children from the age of 5 years, up to the age of 20 years, who are sending letters to me steadily. Take, for instance, one that *Collier's* has picked. It's from a girl of 14 who says, "I have asked my mother and others *why* I was born. When I read your book I realized *what* I was born for. I've organized a group of children my own age and a little older and we're going to study your book and we're going to *live* it."

---

the rising number of claims of psychic contacts with formless 'space' entities, Adamski refrained from distinguishing between the dense-physical manifestation of life on Earth and the etheric-physical nature of life on the other planets in the solar system. See also Appendix II.

6 Here Adamski refers to the Indochina conflicts as a result of the French — and later American — occupation. The truth of his statement can also be seen in the unstoppable migration of people whose societies and economies have been colonized by, first industrialised countries, and then mega-corporations for cheap raw materials and labour, following the institutionalization of global inequality through the Bretton Woods institutes (World Bank, GATT, WTO, IMF).

7 *Collier's* was a weekly national interest magazine, published from 1888 until 1957.

The interests of our children in general are, today, in space. And don't forget one thing. We've already made one great statement that we're going to put out a satellite — and that's not going to be the only one. There will be many! As we go further into space we'll be in the same category that Galileo was in his time. When Galileo built his telescope and looked into the heavens, he said that the Heaven that was taught to him from childhood was not there, but there were other planets. Immediately he was stepped on!

He was able to carry on until he became an old man, then he was stepped on altogether and had to refute everything he had said in order to live. We know that history. We are in that same position today, believe it or not. We have forces that have been fighting this. I was on Steve Allen's television show when I was in New York recently and I was told, "Don't let anyone put words in your mouth. We've been told to play this whole thing down." The man didn't say *who* told him.[8]

As for the governments — whether it be this one or any other — you cannot look to them and expect to get the *truth*. The *have* it! But, they cannot give it. First the people must be educated. WHAT PEOPLE DO NOT UNDERSTAND — THEY FEAR! If the governments come out it will be on the hostile side as it was in France. I have a French paper that says there isn't a diplomat in the French government who doesn't know something about Space People. Last year, after several (saucer) landings, the French peasants went into the woods (with pitchforks) and searched for Space People. As a result they pierced two of their own people — mistaking them for spacemen. The same thing would happen here. So you *must* have education.

---

8 The *Steve Allen Show* was an American variety show on New York's WNBT Channel 4, hosted by Steve Allen from December 1953, until it went on national TV at NBC in 1956. See also pages 46-47.
According to researcher Robbie Graham, "the US government's historical efforts to manipulate UFO-themed media products (...) have affected the content of numerous films and TV products over a six-decade time span" (Graham (2015), *Silver Screen Saucers*, p.16). Other than a tentative effort to test the public reception of a benign extraterrestrial presence with the feature film *The Day the Earth Stood Still* (1951), it resulted in scaremongering crowdpleasers such as *Invaders from Mars* (1953), *Earth vs the Flying Saucers* (1956), *Invasion of the Saucer Men* (1957), et cetera.

The religious groups are responsible! We are facing a condition today like has never been faced in our time. We can go one way or another. We must not kid ourselves anymore! The more we kid ourselves the greater danger we're going to be in. We're at a crossroads, and atomic war could take place. We're not free from it yet regardless of what Russia thinks or how she acts at the moment. *Or*, we can go the other way — the Sky Way, so to speak. As minds turn toward the sky the danger of war lessens towards the ground. For it takes thought — UNITED THOUGHT — to perpetuate anything, whether it's a conflict state or a harmonious state. It's no longer a time to save a man on one corner. It's a time to save the world — from an atomic catastrophe. That's one angle.

The other angle is the young generation. By 1970 the 5-year-old girl will be 20. They're the coming generation. We do not live for ourselves, we live for our children. The boy of 15 will be 30, and so down the line. As these satellites go out more definite information will be gotten. Science will be moving forth through Outer Space. No limits there — and we're bound to improve as we go along. The further we go into space, the further will this great mythical Heaven be away from us. We already know that 1 billion, 500 million stars and planets were discovered by the 100-inch telescope, prior to the 200-inch scope at Mount Palomar. So you can see that we have to go far in distance before there is any sign of an abode like Heaven — as we have been taught. These youngsters *will follow science!* There will be *concrete information* for them. What will happen by 1970 then, if it's a case of fifteen years continuation of (just scientific) research into space? The chances are awfully good — I'm not a prophet — but the chances are awfully good from the way things look now, that the churches will be pretty empty places.

Everything is moving forward now, into space. We can grow to be one of the greatest civilizations the world has ever known — by following the present trend of things into outer space — or we can go to oblivion by an atomic war. It's our choice and I believe that if the ministry, to which the people look to most for information, were to comply with biblical history AS IT'S WRITTEN — it doesn't have to be interpreted — and begin to speak in those terms and at least admit that there is a fulfillment of some prophecies, it would alert the people on the honorable side, or the reverent side. The things would begin to come down to some real basis of understanding and would eliminate the danger and fears of the world itself — the responsibility is upon their shoulders!

For instance, you all ask, "Why doesn't Eisenhower speak out?" "Why doesn't So-and-So speak out?" When I was in Mexico City, the Minister of Information said to me, "Look George, I can come out any morning with new information as we get it," and they do not put it out pretty freely. "But," he added, "If I do, the opposition will come out the next day in the paper and say, 'This man is no longer fit for office. He's flying around in flying saucers.' Yet I can work through you. They may pounce on you but they won't pounce on me." And that's what happened, I have a copy, in Spanish, of the lecture which I gave there. Our own ambassador was there . . . If President Eisenhower[9] told you the truth — which he has — if he ran for re-election next year he'd be beaten — by the very people who, today, would elect him. Because the opposition would throw that in his face. EVERY government has the truth, not only ours. Russia has started bending her knees pretty well through many things — and if the truth could be told right now you'd be amazed at what the Space People have already done! But you can see, these men, after all, have positions. Unless they can get the backing of a total population they can't come out as one-individual targets.[10]

The same is true of the ministry. It's up to the people to ask the ministry for that information. A minister is working under someone else and so on down the line. It's an organized institution. Many ministers would have brought out a lot of wonderful things already, because many of them are well-informed. But they wonder how the congregation is going to take it. They must comply with the majority of their congregation. Otherwise they might find themselves without jobs, and they, too, have to live.

---

9 Dwight D. Eisenhower, US president from 1953-1961. See also pages 1-5.

10 See also Adamski's answers on pages 74-75 about the general public accepting the reality of the extraterrestrial presence.

We're living in that kind of a world. The situation then, is very *critical* and very broad in some fields and it means that humanity, itself, to save itself must get together and have an *understanding* with each other. *That's* the present condition.

Prior to the Geneva Conference[11], our newspapers carried a list of the subjects that would be taken up during the Four Power Conference there. I have an article that came out in the [Los Angeles] *Examiner* saying that the Powers would discuss conditions in reference to the people — they did not say space ships, they referred to people — of *other worlds*. As much as to say, *They are here!* If they had not intended to discuss it they would not have included it in that list. So there is PROOF that the Four Powers have considered it. We have other evidence that they talked about space. The Four Powers, themselves, must have agreed as to when to release the information in reference to a space craft that they, themselves, are going to put out as a satellite.

Remember, when Eisenhower signed that Bill, the other three nations automatically came forth with the same information. So it was agreed upon at the Conference that this information would be let out at that time, beginning here and supported by the other three immediately. So, they have talked about it.

I also have a French pamphlet, 'Interplanetaria' [*Le Courrier Interplanétaire*] which contains an article by professor Alfred Nahon.[12] I cannot read French so it was translated for me. This article deals with what took place at the Geneva Conference — and, in a way, with what the space people have already *done* that's beneficial to this Earth. It's very interesting.

I have another letter here also showing that the movement is wide. It's from a Mr. Godette (who is mayor of Bonn, Germany). Before I came on this trip, he was brought to my home by Mayor Carr of San Diego, Secret Servicemen and Congressman Fletcher. We had a short talk and later he wrote and asked for some of my pictures,

---

11 On 18 July 1955 the world's 'Big Four', i.e. the United States, the Soviet Union, Great Britain, and France, convened the Geneva Summit to reduce the global tensions and mistrust that were building during the Cold War.

12 Alfred Nahon (1914-1990), founder of the Association Mondialiste Interplanétaire (AMI) and editor of *Courrier Interplanétaire*.

which I sent to him. Then I received another letter form him telling me about the International Council of Christian Leadership that is being organized in Germany. A picture was enclosed showing a castle that they are rebuilding.

He is the head of this group and tells how many people have already attended their meetings. He hopes that I can some day go to Germany and give a lecture there. Mr. Godette says he worked along with me I work right along with him, whether I know it or not.

There is a woman who flew here from Africa, where she owns a big plantation. She came to see me to find out what is really happening. When she returned to Africa she started a group there. So, you can see, the movement is worldwide already.[13] And you can't have a halfway affair. Up to now that's what we've had. From now on we must get the other half in before we can have the unit. That is where the spiritual side, as some people would call it, comes in. I would call it the religious side to bring it to the reverent place where it really belongs. *Then*, the day will come when you won't have to ask me, "What did you find out?" "Were you really there?" "Are there really people there?" No, you might have it then on your weekends at home — enjoying a dinner with Them and They with you.

It's no different, when you get down to brass tacks, than when Columbus came here and discovered this beautiful land on which we've built up so well. He, too, was not actually BELIEVED at the time. There has to be a scapegoat somewhere in the beginning and the pioneer always is, although I don't class myself in that way because I wasn't the first one.

There are a good many cases of contacts but the people didn't have

---

13 Two years later, in 1957, on the advice of his space contacts, Adamski set up the Get Acquainted Program (GAP) in which groups of interested people in over twenty countries were loosely affiliated to receive the latest updates and answers to questions. Although mostly ignored by detractors and others who have documented the flying saucer era of the 1950s and 1960s, the globe-spanning GAP network was highly effective as a pre-internet information sharing network, with the successors to some Japanese chapters still actively meeting to this day. See also: <www.the-adamski-case.nl/his-mission/global-reach/gap/>.

the nerve to tell about it for fear of criticism. And I will tell you honestly that I, too, would not have come out as much as I have, had it not been for that first contact and the four people who where with me — Williamson and the others [Mrs. Williamson and Mr. and Mrs. Bailey], who went to Phoenix Arizona, and gave the story to the [Phoenix] *Gazette*.[14] Once that came out I was on the spot completely and there was nothing else to do. And once you stick you neck out you might as well go ahead with it.

Eventually things come out all right and I'm mighty glad that I've been given the opportunity to do this and to have the strength to do it, because I'm no longer a young man. So long as I can leave something good, even if I do ever so little but it's going to be here for the good of others, why, I'm willing to do it. The time will come for every man and mine will come also. And mine might be much closer than most of yours because of my age. So, I'm doing what I can.

Some people think I'm making a lot of money. You'll be surprised to learn that I took a loss on my first book. It's *not* the money — you can't take it with you, that's one thing. But WHAT YOU CAN DO HERE that will *live* and *help others* is the thing that counts.

Questions and answers

Rev. John Safran (Central Methodist Church, Detroit, Mich.): I'm John Safran, one of the associate ministers at Central Methodist Church. I'm representing Henry Hitt Crane here today. I think it's apparent that Henry Hitt Crane and I have never been afraid of making a statement that we truly believe. Henry Hitt Crane isn't afraid of losing his job and I've never been afraid of losing my job. In fact, they can put me outside here tomorrow morning, on the Cross, if they want to, if I realize that a thing is the truth.

But I want to ask you a question — assuming that I'm a reasonable, sane individual — I know nothing about flying saucers

---

14 See: Len Welch, 'Flying Saucer Passenger Declares A-Bomb Blasts Reason for Visits', *The Phoenix Gazette*, November 24, 1952.

but I have an open mind and I'm willing to learn — Do you think that if you were in my place this morning, that on the basis of what you said in the last 15 to 20 minutes, that you would believe what you want us to believe?

Mr. Adamski: Yes, if I were a Christian, I would — because it's all in the Christian doctrine, as I've mentioned. I've been taught it from childhood on. I'd *have* to believe *that* part regardless of how I looked at it or how I felt about it.[15]

Rev. Safran: On the basis of what you said this morning?
Mr. Adamski: That's correct.

Rev. Safran: May I say this and then I'll remain quiet. I was born a Catholic. At an early age I left the Catholic Church and called myself an atheist. Until 25 I was an atheist. From 25 to 35 I was an agnostic. I don't accept religion unless I experience it! I don't believe in God because any minister told me there's a God. I *experienced* it! I don't believe in flying saucers because you or Henry Hitt Crane or anybody else says it. I've got to experience it!

Mr. Adamski: All right, I'll take your Christian doctrine. I can understand your position very well. I, too, was brought up as a Catholic. I will go this far. A lot of times we ask for things. As the Great Master says, "They will ask for signs but no sign shall be given." You're asking for the same thing that the Christians asked when they wanted Jesus to come off the cross and prove Himself. He did not do that just to prove it to them. You've got to have it *in you*!

You said you were an agnostic at one time and you were also an atheist. NEVER! And I've met a lot of them. Because Man *has* to believe in something.[16] He may not believe in the same God, or in some Church or some religion, but he does believe that he's governed, or is subject unto some Power, though he may not name it.

But the mere fact that he *is* subject unto some kind of power whatever that power may be to his mind; nature, the Sun, the atmospheric condition changes, etc., — he's admitting a power

---

15 See also Adamski's comments on pages 48 and 74-75.
16 The original transcript has: "Because he has to believe in something."

greater than that of his own.

Mrs. Marxer (Study Group of Interplanetary Relations): May I say something on behalf of the study group, Mr. Adamski? Please don't misunderstand us, Rev. Safran, we are not asking anyone to BELIEVE. We are happy to pass on what we have experienced for you to evaluate for yourself, sir. You will admit, even though you might not have had experiences, that does not mean that *other* people have not had them, you see.

Mr. Adamski: It's quite fortunate and yet unfortunate, but on universal grounds — if we had experienced the pains of the Cross, as Jesus did, we probably would have *lived* it. But since we did not experience it we *have not* lived it. As a result, we have had two great wars and a third one about to hover over us. When you wait for experience — sometimes it's a long way off.

Dr. M.E. Gray (Church of Christ, Allen Park, Mich.): Mr. Adamski, I have been in this investigation long enough that I believe in the existence of flying saucers. Some of the things I have heard I find it impossible to believe can claim to come about. I would like very much to believe all that you have said. At the same time, to take the word of one man — alone, without witnesses — the government, the laws of the land will not accept one man's word.

Christ, Himself, didn't ask people to accept that. And, gathered before you are men and women of integrity, sincerity, intelligence and ability. We represent two powerful voices in society, the pulpit and the press. We have dedicated our lives to learning and teaching such Truths as we are able to grasp. Our presence here is evidence of a strong desire on our part to learn the truth about visitors from other planets.

In asking us to accept your word in this matter you are doing that which Jesus, Himself, dared not do. He chose twelve witnesses to be with Him intimately and gave seventy others sufficient evidence to satisfy their doubts; Luke 10. When one of the twelve fell into unbelief, because of doubts, Jesus granted him the privilege of feeling and seeing his hands and his side; John 20:27. We believe that you, as a man, have absolutely no right to expect greater faith in you, on our part, than Jesus expected of his followers.

We, therefore, ask you to give us a fair chance to believe in both you and the 'Brothers' by making arrangements with them to carry us in their ships far beyond the 200 mile fringe of Earth's atmosphere. If they so desire we will board their ships in a remote area and make a landing with them in a fitting public place, protecting them and their ships from detention or abuse, by our fellow men, with our lives.

The one satisfactory substitute for a ride in a space ship would be the testimony of the 'two top government scientists' you claim made one trip with you. We challenge you to give us their names so that we can get them to verify your experience. The necessity of at least two witnesses to *prove* any matter is clearly set forth in Deuteronomy 17:6, Numbers 5:30, II Corinthians 13:1 and I Timothy 5:19, as well as in the laws of our land. We recognize this edict as sound and believe in our hearts that this proposal is both logical and fair. You can here and now prove your own sincerity to us by accepting the challenge.

Mr Adamski: I accept this challenge on these grounds. That I *do* have the proof but I will also limit the condition to this base. *If* the governments, not only our own but of the Allies, *will permit* me to print what I have I *will* print it. Don't forget, religion has its place and so has all civil life — and civil life cannot be jeopardized because somebody wants to prove something from a religious point. There is a time and a place for everything — and I think that your whole Christian doctrine has been placed largely on those grounds which are based, so called, on faith.

The material which I got (a piece of metal from a scout ship), with 2½ billion people in the world I can't carry it in my pocket and convince every person, personally. We're not dealing with a small group, we're dealing with 2½ billion people. I have the analysis of that metal. It was done in Britain and proves beyond a shadow of a doubt that what I have been suspecting as aluminum ships *are* aluminum ships. Unfortunately the analysis was restricted and I *can't* go against *any* governmental restrictions. Here it is for you to read if you want to — yet I couldn't publish it in a book.[17]

I have much information I could talk about. I could make headlines in the press every day if I could release it. *But*, I have *kept my word* to the men who entrusted me that their names would not be revealed and jeopardize their positions at the present time. When conditions clear you'll get all of that and you'll say, 'We were asking a little too early.' You cannot pick the corn off the stalk till it matures. Neither can you act prematurely on any other things as well.

Here is something which I read in New York, just two blocks away from the RCA [Radio Corporation of America] building. It came to me from England — "I was told by an American aeronautics engineer, last week, that a scientist high up in the RCA told him — that it is *now known* that there are over 1,200 people in the United States who WERE NOT BORN THIS PLANET."

When I was in Buffalo, New York, recently, I talked with Oberth[18], the great space-platform and rocket scientist with Bell Aircraft Company. There were a lot of things we talked about that I can't go out and speak of publicly. There are many things that we'd like to bring out. Let me tell you this — you're sincere — and you can, too, have the experience if you but only want to. But you'll have to let something else guide you and *not* the traditional and conventional standards on which man has grown — and which have gone far from nature.

Rev. T.H. Voss (Guardian Lutheran Church, Dearborn, Mich.): I believe, Mr. Adamski, that the crucial issue for Christianity always has been the Deity of Jesus Christ. Would you make a statement

---

17 See also Adamski's comments in 'The World of Tomorrow', pages 96-97; and Aartsen (2022), op cit, 'Exhibit #2: Physical evidence'.

18 Hermann Oberth (1894-1989), Austro-Hungarian-born German physicist and rocket science pioneer who was quoted as saying: "It is my thesis that flying saucers are real, and that they are space ships from another solar system. I think that they possibly are manned by intelligent observers who are members of a race that may have been investigating our earth for centuries" (*The American Weekly*, 24 October 1954). And: "Having weighed all the pros and cons, I find the explanation of flying discs from outer space the most likely one." (*Flying Saucer Review*, Volume 1 Number 2, May–June 1955). See also pages 90-91.

of your convictions from your conversations with the so-called 'Brothers', on the Deity of Jesus Christ?

Mr. Adamski: The word 'Christ' – as we call it to clarify the subject, is a universal thing. It's not denied anywhere in the Universe. The word 'Jesus' is in reference to a human form. Don't forget, even when Peter said, "Thou art the Christ, the Son of the Living God", that Jesus, Himself, made the statement that "Flesh and blood", which was the form of Jesus, as he was known, "hath not revealed it unto thee, but my Father who is in Heaven." Here he made reference to something that *could not* be seen by the human eyes, but he also classified *that* which could be seen — the flesh and blood which was the body of Jesus. So, universally the Christ is accepted. Physically, on the basis of form, they are classified as forms — under whatever name."

Rev. Voss: These questions are not so important but this has always intrigued me. We see in the 70s and 90s of the 1800s there were so many phenomena of this sort. Is there any reason why they are again appearing in this cyclic manner?

Mr. Adamski: Yes, I don't know where we have messed up but we have someplace. Man has mixed things up pretty well from time to time — but, it's this. The calendar has been changed. Just what we lost and where we lost the years, we don't know. But we lost them someplace. If history is correct as to the birth of Jesus, then the 2000 years were over in 1939 and we will be in 2015 tomorrow morning.[19] That also fulfills your prophecy, if you're a good Bible student. The unfortunate part is that we take one portion of the Bible and let the rest of it go by. You've got to study it *all* if you're to understand it all.

But, it tells us that after 2000 years — which they called a dispensation — a new dispensation would enter. That the old would pass away and the new would come.[20] We've had trouble since 1939 and it's not over with yet. It's still moving. Our own government

---

19 According to esotericist Benjamin Creme Jesus was actually born in 24 BCE. See Creme (1993), *Maitreya's Mission*, Vol. Two, p.228.

20 This corresponds with the 'new paradigm' that is now generally seen as inevitable by various UFO/UAP researchers and disclosure activists. See Aartsen (2022), op cit, 'Exhibit #7: New paradigm'.

has changed many times. It changes by the day. Where it's going to stop – your guess is as good as mine. We don't know. But it's moving towards some goal. We go through all kinds of 'isms', phases of all kinds; ideas and one thing or another. Eventually we settle down to some definite point. We'll notice that point pretty well around 1960.

Rev. Voss: Naturally, when we argue theology — perhaps we should not argue it, but we do — we very often suspect that many of the arguments that a man presents are due to his own personal thinking and background. I would like to have you frankly state to us the degree to which your former teaching of Universal Law enters into your present theological viewpoints.[21]

Mr. Adamski: Universal Law is God's Law, if you want to put it correctly. We call it Universal Law, but it's God's Law because there is NOTHING on this Earth or in the Heavens — as you would call them, which are the skies — that a man ever had anything to do with, in the way of creating it. Those bodies are governed by a definite law. Had they not been they would have collided long ago and would have had troubles, as men have been 'collisioned' by living by their own laws.

Therefore, they fit into not only what you call Christian doctrine, but fit, you might say, into a doctrine of Universal Principle. I know of NO race of people who don't worship something in the way of Divine Power. Under different names, yes. But I know of no race that doesn't worship something. Even the American Indians worshipped the future Hunting Grounds.

Mrs. Luzette Sparin (New Thought Alliance, Calif.): Mr. Adamski, you have already answered my question in part, but I wonder if you

---

21 The Reverend is referring here to Adamski's teaching with the Royal Order of Tibet between 1928-1940, as expounded in his books *The Invisible Ocean* (1932) and *Wisdom of the Masters of the Far East* (1936). While seen by most critics and detractors as distinct from his later work, his books about his contact with the space visitors and his later teachings (as in *Cosmic Philosophy*, 1961), as well as his reply to this question indicate that Adamski considered it an integral part of his life's mission.

would add something more to clarify the statement made by Mr. Buck Nelson, that physical adjustments in interplanetary travel are not complex, as we have always believed.

Mr. Adamski: I don't know his experience. I have heard about it but I have never seen or met the man personally.[22] But, let is look at the picture this way. Our Earth at this very moment is revolving at 162 miles per second on one side, that's the orbit side, making around 600 million miles a year. It also revolves at 18½ miles per second on the 24-hour basis, which is sunrise to [sunrise][23]. Do we *know anything* about that movement? No! Not one of us! Why? Because we are living in a sea of air and that air is moving with the Earth as a unit. Just like the fish that knows nothing about the movement and the roughness of the waters upon the surface of the ocean. It's the same idea.

The friction that is to be encountered will be encountered somewhere out there [in space]. Let me explain it this way so you'll all understand. If you place a man on the yolk of an egg he is drowned in the white of the egg.[24] Then, if you throw him, would he know that he's been thrown? No. Because the shell of the egg would encounter the differences as it goes through the air — not the inside of the egg. We are just like that. These people [from other planets] have learned that Law and have built what we might call an artificial planet, known as a space craft. They ride in it and don't feel the movement and speeds don't count anymore than they do right on Earth. It's that simple.

We hooked on to that power in 1920 when we brought in the first crystal sets.[25] You would hook up one wire from your earphones to

---

22 Buck Nelson's contact experience took place in April 1955 and the Michigan Study Group on Interplanetary Relations invited him to speak in Detroit in July 1955, but his book (*My Trip to Mars, the Moon, and Venus*) was only published in 1956. In his 'Word about the Author' Mr. Nelson seems to indicate he met Adamski at some later point when he writes: "… also George Adamski has done much to help me, and he tells the world he believes my story."

23 The original transcript has "sunrise to sunset", which would be only 12 hours.

24 I.e. surrounded by, as we are surrounded by the atmosphere. See also pages 44 and 62.

25 Adamski refers here to the year when the first commercial wireless radio broadcast was transmitted.

one end of the coil wire and you would ground the other wire. Then you had no sound or power — that is, as far as you could detect. But when you took the so-called cat's whisker and touched the galena properly you'd get propulsion because the diaphragms in the earphones began to go into action, vibrating on the little magnets.

Then sound came and power was noticeable. We have become so complicated in some things that now, when simplicity comes it's also complicated to us. That's how simple the program really is — but we threw it overboard for power sets.

And let me say here, our sun is 93 million miles away. Mars will be just 35 million miles away next year. If you figured even an average of 100 million miles to another planet, you could make three round trips a year to a planet if you travelled at the speed of the Earth, 600 million miles a year. And don't think for a minute that we're far from it. Just before I left home the Convair Division[26] announced that we're going to have a ship, probably in 18 months, that will be going from New York to England in 90 minutes. We're just beginning to realize what man *can* do. So, when things start happening — suddenly, as they usually do — all these things will come and there will be many red faces. I have no doubt.

Mrs. Sparin: How can we best prepare to serve this whole problem so that more people, whose influence would be greater in the world, can speak out?
Mr. Adamski: I believe, and I always have believed and the evidence is outstanding — that we have not done our duty by our people in this world, for some reason or another. For, if we had done our duty we wouldn't have suffered and gotten the world that it's in today. I'm referring to the spiritual side of life.[27]

That's where honor really is always acknowledged in full. You honor your fellow man when you *understand* him and that condition can come *only* through the *pulpit*.[28] That's why all the striving from

---

[26] The airplane manufacturing division of General Dynamics Corporation.

[27] Nearly 70 years later, as this compilation goes to press, Adamski's words hold truer than ever.

[28] Spoken before the general secularisation of society.

the other side [sciences, etc.] has not done too much up to now. It has brought a lot of news, anticipation, contradictions, etc., and now only the pulpit can help. For the pulpit is supposed to be the mediator between the Creator and His creation, Man.[29]

If the churches neglect it, all governments will neglect it. Because all governmental officials have been taught from childhood to respect what they are taught in the churches — *that* is the solution. Once things are brought out and put on the reverent side there will be no trouble. We'll have plenty of joys and we'll make *real* progress.

I'd like to tell you something that shows how strange we can be. Some of you may have heard the radio program where they discussed a Bill that will be presented to Congress when they convene again. This is a Bill to add a new Department to the government that will deal with space laws, because no laws have been formulated yet. One Congressman asked, "We have the twelve-mile zone on the ocean. How far out will we go in space?" Another congressman said, "We don't know. We haven't got the same kind of markings out in space as we have on land. But the Moon is part of the Earth. Why not go as far as the Moon?" So it was agreed that we'd go as far as the Moon. A reporter who was also on the program spoke up, "Well, how about the Venusians and the Martians *who are really coming our way at this time?* Will they come under this law?" "Of course they will," was the answer.

We can get so complicated by not adhering to the real truth of things that are happening. A couple of years ago some fellow applied for a charter for outer space. It was in the papers and on radio and television. Everyone laughed at him and called him a crackpot. Well, he *got* the charter. I don't know how, but he did. Then our government announced that they're going to put a satellite out. Two or three days later this man came out and said, "They can't do anything of the kind without getting my permission." And legally

---

29 In present-day society, before the restoration of a true spiritual understanding of life by way of the Ageless Wisdom teaching, the shortcomings of science may be relieved by a post-materialist science that acknowledges a universal consciousness as the foundation of reality, thereby seeking to bridge the existing chasm between science and spirituality. See also the Introduction, pages 16-17.

he's right, since he has that charter.[30] So, you see how tangled up we get by not listening and taking our time and really looking at the picture as it is?

In closing, I will repeat that the responsibility lies with the church leaders, regardless of denomination. And I must admit this. Not because I was reared as a Catholic, please overlook that — but I do have something to report to you. They are moving in the right direction a lot faster than many others. You can see it in the article in *Time* magazine that I mentioned. There is also a book written by Dr. Benjamin Benincasa, of Buffalo, New York, who is the brother of bishop Tio Benincasa. The manuscript is now in the hands of the same lady who proofread my book and will be published by the same publishing company. The title of the book is 'Religions of Other Worlds'.[31]

So, be careful how you criticize from now on because you're liable to be on the wrong side.

---

30 In January 1949 self-help writer James T. Mangan (1896–1970) submitted his claim to all of outer space — 'Charter of Celestia', the Nation of Celestial Space — with the Recorder of Deeds and Titles of Cook County, Illinois, which was duly entered, and in 1958 he applied for membership of the United Nations but was denied. In January 1967 the United Nations adopted the Outer Space Treaty, declaring space free for all nations to explore.

31 In his next talk (September 19, 1955) Adamski refers to the book as *Religions on Other Planets* (see page 50). In the event, it seems Dr Benjamin D. Benincasa (1909-1971) did not manage to find a publisher for his book, as no publications to his name can be found following his Ph.D. dissertation (*The Influence of the spiritual epistles of St. Catharina of Siena*, 1951).

George Adamski often explained the effect of the planet's atmosphere using the analogy of an egg (see pages 40 and 62), as he did here while sharing a meal with local members of the Get Acquainted Program in Auckland, New Zealand during his world lecture tour in 1959.

(Photo: Tony Brunt (2010), *George Adamski – The Toughest Job in the World*.)

Saucers and Religion

Talk by George Adamski

Veteran's Memorial Building
September 19, 1955

Introduction by Laura Marxer (Founder of the Interplanetary Foundation, pioneer saucer researcher, author of Saucers! Simple As A.B.C.[1]*):*
Good evening, ladies and gentlemen. Welcome to a special meeting of the Study Group on Interplanetary Relationships. Before introducing Mr. George Adamski to you, to some of you for the third time, I would like to take just a minute for some announcements.

The study group has been formed to try to make ways and means for individuals to study what has come to us and evaluate it, that is true. But we feel that it is not yet time for study beyond that. We feel that the first mission is to get the visitors in here, and then, all can study. So this is your job to do, too. Nobody but you can do it. It isn't a business of feeling a little disgusted because some Saucer Club is not so active as you would like to have it. It is not a responsibility of a few officials of any group. IT IS YOUR JOB. If you aren't happy with the little bit of saucer information that you see in the newspapers, then it is your own fault. Write to the newspapers (and I suggest that you write to the *managing editors*, not the city editors, because the city editors have bosses too) and tell them that you *know* that there is more saucer information and ask why they aren't printing it in the newspapers. Or, write to your President, or to your congressman, or get to your religious leaders and spiritual advisors. What we are trying to set up with these forthcoming public lectures tomorrow night and Wednesday night[2] is an opportunity to

---
1 See Appendix I, page 113 ff.
2 No transcript of the lecture on Wednesday September 21, 1955 is known to have been distributed.

bring together the Clergy and the individual. Some ministers want to go into this, but they are afraid of their congregation, and vice-versa. The first mission is to bring about a public disclosure of the existence of flying saucers and visitors — and nobody but you and I are going to do this. This is upon the people themselves.

Tonight Mr. Adamski has said that he will touch upon the spiritual aspect of the flying saucer situation. The question and answer period will follow as usual after intermission.

And now, it is certainly my pleasure to introduce to you, Mr. George Adamski.

George Adamski (Co-author of Flying Saucers Have Landed, *author of* Inside the Space Ships, *lecturer, philosopher):*
Thank you very much.

The question of flying saucers has been thrashed in and out, but I say that *it is of no value at the moment!* That is quite a statement to make but that is the truth. Because, you might say, when a man knocks on the door so many times, once that door has been opened, what is the sense of knocking any more? And that door has been opened!

I got many letters asking me when am I going to start a class of one kind or another. I am told that most of you are students, and the question in everyone's mind seems to be, "What can I do?" That is the point we are going to take up tonight.

First, I want to read you a letter that I got today from the same lady who sent in the report of a crashed saucer to Dorothy Kilgallen's column.[3] She says, "There is a lot of fun being made of a lot of things down here now. The flying saucer headlines are being squashed at this time, but things are moving faster and there are more saucers this year than at any time before." I can go along with that because when I was on Steve Allen's television show recently, I met the man who was in charge of the program when I was on it two years ago.

---

3   Dorothy Kilgallen (1913-1965) was an American columnist and journalist with the *New York Evening-American*, and a TV personality.

He told me, "George, watch your step. They are going to try to trap you. So don't let anyone put words in your mouth. We've been told that the press, radio, and television must play this thing down."[4] So I know there is such as a game going on. And yet I had the finest reception in New York this time. Everyone cooperated on both the *Steve Allen Show* and the *Morning Show*. We didn't let things get too serious because those programs go out to the general public and had to be a little light. It is hard to know how the public is going to react. I have a letter from a lady in Cleveland who says that her little boy was watching me on the Morning Show and said, "Look, Mama, Mr. Adamski says we don't have to be afraid of these space people." This woman hadn't realized that her son was afraid, but when he said that she remembered that they had seen some movie about hostile space people. The child must have been frightened but hadn't said anything until he heard me. That fear is not only in a little child — it is a common fear among people in general. And they can't be blamed for it altogether because, after all, WHAT THEY DON'T UNDERSTAND, THEY FEAR!

I said that the saucers are no longer the dominant factor in this. They have brought their message through, you might say, even if they have not spoken. They have alerted the world at last — and I say the *whole* world because I get information from all parts of the world — to the one thing that the world has never thought of before. And that is that we are not alone in the Universe. Even the great skeptics, while they may not believe you and me, are still looking into the sky, wondering when they are going to see something. They have been alerted to the idea that at least it is possible. The potentials are there, if nothing else.

So, they have alerted the whole world to the idea that there is more in the sky than there is on the Earth and that the Earth is not alone. It is the same as when Columbus came to this country. Nobody believed him — that there was anybody on this piece of land. Yet here we are. And when he came there were just a few people. There

---

4   See also page 28, note 8.

were no cities or anything like that.[5] Indians were well satisfied — we disturbed that peace — and out of that disturbance came the great civilization that we have today in our own beautiful nation.

But we are heading for another mess! Science has said many times that in case of atomic warfare we could be annihilated as a civilization. So, we might say, we are at a cross-roads at this time, and it is up to us to decide which road we will take. If we take the road we've been taking, then destruction is awaiting us! If we withdraw from that road and start looking skywards toward something we can learn that we have not known before[6], we will lessen the cause of destruction *by not supporting it*.[7]

We find that these people have knocked on our door when we least expected it although they have been traveling over the Earth steadily, but seldom landing. We have not made very much progress according to their statements. They tell me that some 2000 years ago they made appearances on the Earth and found that men were slaughtering their fellow man. Now, 2000 years later, they have returned and found the same conditions, except on a larger scale and with more modern methods. This proves that we have not yet learned the Brotherhood of Man or the Fatherhood of the Creator.

You may ask, "Why don't more people believe in the saucers?" You cannot expect people to believe in the saucers or the coming of the space people. They haven't believed the Christian teachings. When a man believes something he lives it.[8] The reason those of you who are students of metaphysics or any other kind of study (it doesn't make any difference what it is) are floundering is because you have *never believed* that you have been taught. If you even once apply just a *minute* part of the knowledge that you may posses to actual living, without going fanatically off the beam, you will realize

---

5 I.e. in the modern sense. Recent research shows that various early native civilizations lived in large settlements that classify as cities.

6 I.e. international cooperation towards peaceful resolution of conflict.

7 Within a few years after these early warnings against the threat of nuclear warfare, the public began to oppose the nuclear option, which led to the establishment of the Campaign for Nuclear Disarmament in the UK in 1958.

8 See also Adamski's comments on pages 34, and 74-75.

a great difference in life. A lot of people ask me, "Why do you take so much interest in this? Are you afraid that when you die you may not go on to where you want to go if you do not?" No, I am not afraid of the Hereafter. The Hereafter is not the question. What can I learn *here* and *now*, I can also enjoy; so, I have already received my reward. HE WHO KNOWS MUCH ABOUT LIFE, GETS MUCH OUT OF LIFE. HE WHO KNOWS NOT ANYTHING ABOUT LIFE, DOESN'T EVEN KNOW HE IS LIVING! So, what we *learn* is a reward in itself.

You have heard many fantastic ideas, and mine is just as fantastic probably as others, but one thing is sure — I am not organizing anything. I have no organisation and don't intend to. I will stay free as I am. I will render my service wherever it is asked for, but that is all. I'm not out for anything for myself. Yet I could organize, because there are about 20 million people who are writing to me now. Last week over 2000 letters were sent to my home. It is quite a job for those at home to answer all that mail, but they do answer every letter. I could easily organize and become a very rich man. All I would have to do is ask for a dollar per person. With 20 million people I have 20 million dollars just like that. I wouldn't have to work, to lecture or write books — I could enjoy riding around in a Cadillac. But, *there is a job to be done*. We are challenging the religious leaders of the world. And it is beginning not only here. It is already started in Africa, as well as in other places. A lady flew in from Africa and came to my home for one purpose, to learn about the flying saucers. She was so interested that she took the information back and began to get it to the people there as well.

What are our spiritual leaders actually going to do about the flying saucer situation? As students, giving thought to your development, for the betterment of yourself, your community, and the Universe, analyze it for yourselves. The teachers of Metaphysics, Christianity, Mohammedanism, Hinduism, Buddhism, etc., all tell you that there is a Hereafter. But they tell you that *you must die to get there.* Yet Jesus, who was flesh like you and me and was born in this world said, "I am in this world but not of it."[9] We are told that

---

9   See John 17:13-14.

after the abusing of His body, He took that body up into Heaven, which has always been considered skyward, proving one thing — if you had a way of getting there, you could go up with this body and go on living. Then we were told about two years ago that the Virgin Mother also went that way. Jesus said, "In my Father's house are many mansions. I go to prepare a place for you that you may also be there." He called this world a mansion also, proving that there is no difference there than here. It is solid foundation, in other words. We are told in many Biblical statements that certain individuals were taken away from here in fiery chariots. They, too, went into the sky somewhere and they have not returned. It was probably better there than here — they enjoyed it and stayed. The Lord's Prayer says, "Thy will be done on earth as it is in Heaven." How do you suppose we are going to establish anything on earth like it is in Heaven unless somebody from Heaven comes our way and tells us what is to be done? Then we are told that in these latter days the Son of Man will be coming from the sky, or Heaven, to earth.

All of this *is* happening! What are our spiritual leaders going to say about that? If they say, "there is nothing to it, we don't believe it," then they must admit that they have been feeding us a little fairy story. So, it is up to them. There will be a book out pretty soon entitled, "Religion on Other Planets". This book was written by Dr. Benjamin Benincasa whose brother is a Papal Secretary of State. I have met these men and was told that the book speaks of flying saucers.[10] This is quite a forward step.

The Council of Churches has interviewed me, and a representative of the Archbishop of Canterbury of England came and talked to me. So the interest is there. The question now is, are *you*, regardless of your denomination, interested? The Ministry is wondering about you — how are you going to take it if they speak up? If you rebuke them, they can lose their jobs which is something they cannot afford to do. If you *demand* the truth from them, and if enough people voice that demand, then they can come forward. I know of about 600 ministers who want to do this. There is a minister in Iowa City

---

10   See also page 43, note 31.

who even told his superiors that he was going to quit his job to be free to lecture on this. But they told him, "No, we don't want you to quit. We want you to be right where you are to give what you have to the public, because the public has been asking for the truth." The flying saucer picture is not religious in the sense that some people like to misconstrue it, but religious implications are involved. This does not belong solely to any occult group, or any kind of a group, anywhere. It belongs to the world. *It is Universal*, and it should be handled in that manner!

What I have written in my book[11] is very, very little in comparison to all I have really been told — in regard to what is going on. Professor Alfred Nahon[12] told me some months ago that he was introducing a Bill to the French Parliament, through [French Prime Minister] Mendès France, for recognition at the Geneva Conference. On July 17 that Bill was lined up with all the topics that would be discussed at the Conference. It was listed on the agenda that was published in the newspapers, and it would not have been included there if it had not been accepted. We know that they talked about space ships and space, for it was only a week after our space satellite announcement. The other three powers followed with simultaneous announcements.[13] The timing was perfect.

Let me show you how the Force works here. Those of you who have studied much want information. You want signs. You want facts. I don't know how you can get those facts, if these are not facts. I wrote the manuscript of my book just as it was given to me. It was proofread by Charlotte Blodget and then published. I had no idea the timing was so fine that the book would come out about the same time as the announcement of our space satellite. Now, *who* timed it? You want demonstrations — there is one. I couldn't have timed it, for I knew nothing about President Eisenhower's announcement. Yet the Brothers (and we call these people from other planets Brothers because they are of the same Creator as we)

---

11 *Inside the Space Ships*, Abelard-Schumann, 1955.
12 See page 31, note 12.
13 See also page 25.

must have known very well just how to run the show. They did run it perfectly and hit the nail right on the head.

Someday the truth will be known publicly that we have been spared from annihilation three different times by the Brothers. The Korean War was ended by their act. Formosa[14] is messed up so badly that there might have been a war started there. The French Indochina War was side-tracked by Mendès France. How? If you think back a little, you will remember that the war was to begin on the 26th of that month. On the 24th Mendès France asked for a nine-power conference in France. Prior to that you read that around the middle of the year there were about seven landings, personal contacts, made in France by different individuals. One was on a railroad track. What did these Brothers who came down tell these different people during these different contacts that brought Mendès France, an unknown man, from underground to be a famous man in the world?[15] Then he made that demand! I have a French paper at home that says there isn't a diplomat in the French Government who does not know something about space people. So, they must have been told something. He acted at the right time. The Conference was held by the nine powers and some agreements were made that side-tracked the French Indochina conflict and quieted it down. Mendès France, himself, became a big man. The Bill that professor Nahon introduced at the Conference was in behalf of space *people*, not space ships. That is an admission that they are among us. If we can't trust them now, knowing all they have done for us, we will never be able to trust anyone!

Some of you may have heard the radio program the day before our Congress adjourned when they discussed a Bill that will be presented when they convene. This is a Bill to add a new department to the government that will institute some sort of space laws, because no laws have been formulated yet. One congressman asked, "We have

---

14 Present-day Taiwan.
15 Interestingly, after only eight months in office Pierre Mendès France's tenure as Prime Minister of his country ended when his Cabinet fell in February 1955.

the twelve-mile zone on the ocean, but how far will we go in space?" The congressman who drew up the Bill answered, "We don't know, we haven't got the same kind of markings out in space as we have on land. But the Moon is part of the Earth so we'll go as far as the Moon." A reporter who was also on the program spoke up, :"How about the Venusians and the Martians *who are really coming our way at this time?*" Will they come under this Law?" "Of course they will," was the answer. How much more of an admission do you want that things are moving our way when statements like that are made by officials? If you are looking for Eisenhower to make a statement, he is not going to make one. He would be a fool if he did, and he's a smart man. Nor will anyone else in the Pentagon make any individual statements. But collectively they are liable to. Actually, they did just that, because it took the Four Major Powers to support Nahon's Bill; and they did that when they agreed upon the simultaneous announcement of the satellite. You have to read between the lines.

If Eisenhower or any government official were to tell what he knows, do you think he'd be re-elected?[16] No! The people would say, "Well, we can't have him or his party, he's riding around in space ships now." You would be amazed at what the opposition would do. You have to read between the lines. In Mexico the Minister of Information told me, "George, every day I could tell the people something about flying saucers. But if I did, the opposition would say in the next morning's papers, 'We can't have this Minister any more. Now he's riding around in flying saucers. Something is wrong in his upper storey.' But I can work through you."[17] It is the same

---

16 See also pages 1-4 and page 30.
17 From 1954 onward Adamski regularly visited Mexico to give lectures, and returned there almost every year during the winter months until his last visit in January 1965, a few months before his death. His information was well-known in Latin America — even before the publication of *Flying Saucers Have Landed* (1953) Adamski wrote about meeting with a commanding officer in the Chilean air force (see Gerard Aartsen (ed., 2022) *George Adamski – Letters to Emma Martinelli*, p.93). For decades the air force of several Latin American countries have been rather more open about their pilots observing non-terrestrial craft. Tellingly, only in France and Chili did the Rockefeller-sponsored Unidentified

here. You see, the thing is quite ticklish. The governments of the world have gone as far as they can go, so don't look for anything greater from them.

Now the second half must come up and meet this first half. This would be the so-called spiritual or religious side. The churches have a responsibility, a very great responsibility, which I will show to you. This part must now come forth before you will have the full truth. Three major religions are already very interested. A lady showed me a pamphlet put out by a Catholic priest, Father Baker, who built a big cathedral in Lackawanna, near Buffalo, New York.[18] In it he tells that Adam was not born on this Earth but was brought here from another planet. That is something odd for a Catholic priest to say, so I asked the lady to get a pamphlet for me. It is a good thing to have. So you see, a gradual branching out by the churches is taking place. They are testing the public. They are testing the path. It will come sooner or later, and the quicker the better.[19] We need it badly, right now. We are, today, thinking in terms of space on the satellite base alone, but one thing is definite — an incident could take place and global war could flare up. Then it would be too late to do anything about it. So the time is short. As far as the fulfilment of the prophecies are concerned, *they are being fulfilled!*

These people from other planets live as we do. They are not different than you and I, not one iota. They are better looking because they don't live the tense life that we do. They don't struggle for every-day living, so they look better and they stay younger. They don't have any diseases or sickness of any kind. But, as far as being super-human beings, *they are not!* They are like you and me. They have learned more about Life and *applied* it, but we have failed to learn or believe even the teachings of Jesus! For that which man believes, he *lives*.

The evidence is outstanding that we have not believed Jesus

Flying Objects Briefing Document of 1995 receive serious attention.

18 Father Baker (1842-1936) was a Catholic priest known for his national charity fundraisers and building the Our Lady of Victory Basilica in Lackawanna, NY.

19 See also the Introduction, pages 7-9.

or we would have lived His teachings. And since we have not lived them, we have had two major wars and a third one threatening! It is not a matter of *hearing* words. It is taking *those* words, taking *that* knowledge, and putting it to work *by living it.* You say sugar is sweet because you have been told that, but if you have never tasted that sugar, you will never know *how* sweet it is. That is where our trouble really is. Those of you who are students in various fields such as Metaphysics, etc., you have probably failed because you have never applied to life that which you have learned. *And it is time to learn!* Let me show you how simple it really is. You don't even have to have a teacher. All you have to do is analyze *yourself.* You can learn much from your own self!

People ask me, "What is mental telepathy? Why can't we start a class and learn?" There is really nothing to learn. If mental telepathy, as we call it, were not a fact, you would not be here listening to me and I would not be talking to you. That is how simple it is. We overlook the simple things. We look for hard things and we get hard knocks in return. There is no person here who has never received a thought in a loud form as you hear my voice now. The very words that I put to you now first come to me in silent form. If you didn't have that silent form manifesting through you, you would never have been born. You would not be living today. Most people who study try to make more out of something than there is, but when you look at the picture straight, without myth around it, you find that all life about you, independent of yourself, lives by a silent manifestation. Impressions always come silently. Your feeling is not noisy. Your conscience is not noisy, and that conscience never sleeps. Impressions are constantly coming. The trouble with us is we have failed to develop it while others *have* developed it. We have it and don't know it. So, accidently sometimes we accept a few impressions and put them into words and convey them to others. You don't have to be a saint with wings on your shoulders to have it. You can and should live a normal life. Jesus did. All the others did. They didn't go to extremes. We make fun of the savages who may not be living the kind of life we are with radio, TV, automobiles, etc., but they can send a message 1000 miles and receive one without any other means but impressions. *Nature is all silence.* If you give a little more thought to it and give it more strength by recognition, these impressions will come through more often and you will act upon them more often. Then you will realize for the first time that *there is no limit* to how far you can go!

Distance, itself, is not involved at all. How many times has this happened to people? You have a relative or a mother 800 miles away from here. You haven't written to her for about six months. You haven't heard from her, so you figure everything must be all right or they would have written you, and you don't worry. Then something happens at the other end. You may be very busy, perhaps doing a very important job that you must keep your mind on, and you have no time for anything else. Yet you will think of the name of that person or mother. You hadn't even been thinking about mother, but this thought keeps persisting. By the time the day is over you are worried and you begin to wonder, to speculate, if Mother is sick. Has something happened to her? Why am I so impressed with her name upon my mind, or why do I feel her presence around me? A few days later you may receive a letter or a wire telling you that she has passed away, and at the last moment she thought strongly of you. Or it may be a letter saying that she had been sick and thought she couldn't pull through and was thinking of you, but now she is all right. You got her message from a distance of 800 miles. Most people have had such an experience. You can't go through life without having some experiences of that nature at one time or another. That is all there is to mental telepathy. It is recognizing impressions that come.[20] *Give them expression later if you care to, or keep them to yourself.*

People ask me, "How can we commune with the Brothers?" You have already done so, but you fail to recognize it. You cannot have a thought without that thought agitating all of space, any more than you can drop anything in a body of water like an ocean without the whole ocean being affected. You have already been well accepted, or thought of, by them as well. But maybe the reason you haven't

---

20 See also Adamski's course *Telepathy – The Cosmic or Universal Language* (1958).

received anything is because you did not *believe* your thought went out. So you still try to send it out. When you try too often, you get tense and tired and you weaken the force that should be behind it. All of these things are very clear and very simple. We have put names to them such as hunches, premonitions, clairvoyance, clairaudience; but the commonest form that we usually use is touch. Touch is a feeling — you feel something. Feeling is what? A state of alertness — you are alerted to something.[21] Give it a little time and that something will clear itself for you, and then you will know what you have been alerted to. If you don't give it time it will be a myth. Let it alone and it will unfold naturally and will be beautiful. Try to unfold it and you will ruin it. Patience is very necessary in this type of development. Touch is feeling, feeling is alertness, and alertness is what? Consciousness! Lose any of those phases I have mentioned and you lose consciousness. It is really the "quickening of the mind" that the Bible speaks of. It is becoming interested in things greater than that which is around you. It is perceiving them and *taking time* for their revelation, so that you may not completely confuse or put some cloak of myth around them which later would be hard to solve. *Let growth be natural!*

These people who are travelling our way are using that as their means of communication, and it is not much different than the savage who sends and receives a message from a thousand miles. These people have developed the natural qualities of their being, and even they are not fully developed. They tell me that they, too, have a long way to go, for Eternity knows no end to a road. So they will keep going. We have had that *same* opportunity and should have been at their stage long ago. But we seldom trust ourselves. We cannot trust the other fellow because we don't trust ourselves. We cannot have faith in the other fellow if we have none in ourselves. I can illustrate this very simply. If someone were to project a picture of a three dimensional form of a man or woman walking

---

21 'Feeling' here is probably best understood as 'sensitivity' or 'awareness', rather than emotions of 'feeling sad', 'feeling happy', et cetera. In his correspondence with a student Adamski argued that 'touch' stands apart from the other human senses, or might be seen as the 'cardinal sense', fundamental to the other four. See: Aartsen (ed., 2022), op cit, pp.50-52.

down the aisle of this hall, all eyes would see it and all eyes would acknowledge it. But since no sound had been produced of anyone walking on that floor, what would your ears say? "Now, eyes, don't fool me. Don't use your imagination too much. If there were anyone walking across that floor I would have heard him. Since I heard no sound, it must have been your imagination." The ears would judge and condemn. Reverse the situation and reproduce a sound of someone walking across the floor, but no form there, and the ears would accept it and the eyes would condemn it. You see, they don't respect one another. They don't have faith in one another. The sense of smell and the sense of taste are the same. "Man, know thyself and you shall know all things." You must analyze yourself carefully. These people have learnt that. They have learned to harness the wild forces which make up the human being.

You are known for what? You are known for a nose, eyes, ears and mouth. If you didn't have them, there would be no reason for a head. If you didn't have a head, you would be called something else, but not a human being. So, you are recognized as a man by those four characters which are predominant in life. As we go through life they are likely to be attracted by other effects and lean towards other effects because they, themselves, are effects. Ears are attracted by sound, nose by smell, mouth or palate by taste. You will notice I am eliminating one. Since you are students I will give you the law and you can practise from now on. You don't have to go anywhere — just utilize this law, *and work slowly,* and it will come through. It will cost you nothing. Look at the picture in this way. These combined senses are what is called 'carnality'. It is born with the body and there is a death to it. Carnality was born to die. That is the Free Will of man. The eyes, the ears, the palate, and the nose exercise the free will. They are governed by what they see and what they do right here — an effect to an effect. Seldom do you give any thought to *that* which *perpetuates* them — to what makes you operate. That Something is what we call Touch or feeling. Start analyzing THAT! Notice how powerful Feeling is, and you will know how important it is. We have missed this truth and that is why we are confused.

There is not a person in this world who can construct a human body or any other kind of form, and have it function as it does. There is a Character (I'll call him a Character) wo knows what to do when conception takes place for a form to be. He works independent of the form from which that other form will be born. After a few months that little form will turn. As it does, the mother says, "The baby turned." This proves that she was not alerted to this new form until the turn took place. And she didn't get it by any sound, but by touch. It was silent. She got it silently. The form turned silently.

Consider a man building a house. He builds the house and then puts in the windows and the doors last. This house we will call a human being — the eyes, nose, ears and mouth are all put in the same way. Now, notice, they are all born. They are part of the body. That is the carnal part of you and me. But there is an individual Character in there who knew what to do to produce the body. *That one we never looked at.* As a result, these four children were produced in this house start running wild and accusing each other of false imaginations. How in the world can you get a true conception of anything if one is opposing the other?

A violin is a good example of this. There are four strings on it. If those strings are in tune you get harmony when you strike a bow on them. We are striking a bow all the time on our "four strings", but what kind of a sound are we getting — quite a messy affair. As a result, the world is in quite a messy state. But you can tune those strings to each other and make them behave by respecting one another and working as a unit. Then the Master Hand strikes the strings and a beautiful melody, LIFE, comes forth instead of distorted sound, DEATH. When that happens, these senses give up some of their independency, and automatically they give up their free will unto the Will of that One Great Master who has built and given birth. I will show you how important this one thing is, and it is that for which everyone is looking. Many teachers never bring it out in clear form, and naturally, the student doesn't get it straight. We are told, "Man, know thyself and you shall know all things." If you *did* know yourself, you *would* know all things, because this Character builds not only you — he builds the tree, the world, everything. I call Him a Character because He is a single ray in each form, while He comes from a total source called Divine.

Let us say that we have a person in the audience who has eyes that can see TV pictures that are floating around in space without the aid of a TV set. The same person develops his hearing so that he hears the music that follows the program without ever having an instrument to reproduce it. He has the other senses developed to a point where he can smell a flower that has not yet been born, but will be born in the next six months. He tastes the apple that is somewhere in the making but not yet mature and not manifested on the tree. We would say he is a super-human being, wouldn't we? Naturally we would. This man possesses things like no man on earth has ever possessed. But if he doesn't have the thing commonly called touch, or feeling, he is a dead *hombre* and will be buried under six feet of sod. We have people in the world today who have lost these four senses through accidents, etc., but they have this thing called touch; and because they *do* have it they build empires! This proves that this Character can live independent of the four senses, but the four senses cannot live independent of this Character. Right there is your proof of Who is the Boss. So, look to the Big Boss who has been living in this house[22] all the time but was never recognized, and you will get somewhere!

That is what the people of other planets have done — THAT'S ALL. When they got *that* knowledge, they had the knowledge of their Creator. This Character is a speck of the Supreme Creator[23] that created the Universe that manifests and precedes all forms. Forms do not come by themselves. Forms are brought forth by a Greater Intelligence than the form is capable of possessing right now. So the Something that we call Feeling which is a state of alertness, or conscious consciousness, precedes the little form at the time of conception to build it up and reproduce it on earth as Man. That is what Peter recognized in Jesus. When Jesus returned from a journey He asked His disciples, "Who do the people say that I am?" The disciples told Him the people thought he was some Prophet

---

22 I.e. in the human body.
23 I.e. the divine spark, or the human soul that takes incarnation to manifest itself in the three-dimensional world of physical existence in order to spiritualize matter.

returned or reborn. He realized that the people didn't know who He was, so He figured, "These are My disciples. I've educated them — brought them up from fishermen of fish to fishermen of men. They should know because they have been closer to Me." So He asked them directly. They all stood dumbfounded and didn't know what to say. Simon Bar-Jonah, known as Peter, finally spoke up and said, "Thou art the Christ, the Son of the Living God." That was all he said, but Jesus immediately acknowledged it and confirmed it.[24] In Jesus' next words you will find the *Key* that the Catholic Church claims. It is a Universal Key for *everyone* to have, regardless of your denomination, *if* you can grasp it. Jesus said, "Flesh and blood (which is the effect that has been born into the world) has not revealed this unto thee," (everybody judged Jesus from the flesh and blood angle, which is why they called Him various returned prophets), "but My Father which is in Heaven. Upon this rock I will build My Church, and the gates of hell shall not prevail against it." This means exactly one thing; that upon this Truth I will build this physical body up, and nothing in this world will ever go against it!

This is the absolute Truth, and the body couldn't be born without it. You say, "Well, Peter called Him Christ, but what are we? We are not Christ." I believe we *are* as much Christ as the disciples were. I don't know how you feel but I believe that, because Jesus said to the disciples, "I feed you with milk and not with meat, for you are babes in Christ." That single ray that we call *feeling* or *consciousness* is really the Life Force and the Master that builds this temple. That is why you shall know all things when you know yourself for your *real* self. That Force built the Universe and is manifesting through the Universe. It is that simple when you look at the picture correctly. People on other planets have learned this. As a result, they learned another thing through it. Our Bible says, "There is nothing hidden that shall not be revealed." They don't have the same Book that we have, but they do have the same kind of Law.

Our so-called smart people who are only beginning to learn some of the answers ask, "How can the saucers move so fast? How can they

---

24 See Matthew 16:13-17.

make such sharp turns?" I ask these people this, "How come you are living on this Earth?" At this very moment the Earth is speeding through space at 162 miles a second on the orbit side, and 18½ miles a second[25] on the twenty-four hour basis. It has the wobbly system in which makes the sharp turns. Do we know anything about it? Not at all. We don't know a thing about it. Why? Because we are no different than the fish that are in the ocean. They don't know anything about the roughness on the surface of the ocean. We are living in a sea of air that moves with the earth as the earth moves. If we could get out to the fringe of our atmosphere, we would know the difference. We couldn't take it. There is no jet engine behind the earth, no one is pushing or pulling it; but the whole thing is moving. And it is going about 600-million miles a year. On an average of one hundred million miles between the other planets and the earth, we could make *three* round trips to any of those planets in one year, which is not as long as they one time thought it would take to go there. Yet we can move even faster than that. A lot faster. Let me explain it this way so that you may all understand. Everyone knows what an egg is like. Compare the yolk, which is the solid part of the egg, with the Earth. The white of the egg compares with the atmosphere and the shell compares with the fringe of our atmosphere. Put a man on the yolk. He is going to be drowned in the white of this egg, so to speak. Then take the egg and throw it. Would the man know that he has been thrown? Of course not. The shell encounters the differences as it goes through the air — which is exactly what happens to us. It is also the reason we don't feel we are moving at great speed.[26]

That is what these [space] people have learned. They went back to Nature, or to God, call it what you will, and we have to go there to really find the powers that can be harnessed to serve man. We *can* do this because God never denies His off-spring anything. *We* deny ourselves all the things we do not have. This power has motivated the Earth and all the other bodies in space ever since they were created. Some bodies are much bigger than our own Earth. Jupiter

---

25 I.e. nearly 30 kilometres per second.

26 See also pages 40 and 44.

is eleven times bigger. These people have harnessed that power by studying God's Laws instead of man's — Nature's Laws instead of man's. They have built a ship, which is an artificial planet known as a spaceship, and they travel in it.[27] Actually, you could sit on top of that ship. You don't have to be inside. We are sitting on top of the Earth, we are not inside it. We are space people already, and we came from space originally. Where else could we come from?

Outside of space there is nothing. So you could sit on top of a space ship and travel at tremendous speed and never even know you were travelling any more than you do right now. But if you could get out to the fringe of what they call the force field, you would get hurt. You would be blown to bits. They produce this force field artificially.[28] It is like dropping a pebble in a still pool of water. Wavelet after wavelet goes out toward the shore. The primal force where the pebble drops starts the wavelet. That is exactly what they produce around the ship all the time — which is reproducing their atmosphere, their gravity, and everything else. When they come into our atmosphere the wavelets blend. There is no mystery whatever, but they did not solve that through man's calculations. They went to nature and observed their own planet to see how it operates, what causes it to move as it does, and what power makes it move. And they have harnessed *that*!

Naturally, if you are going to learn about anything, you must go to the fellow who produced that thing. In this case, the fellow who produced the planet, and thousands and millions of other planets, is what we have classified as God, or the Supreme Being of the Universe. Who else would know it? The Visitors know that every human being and every form that manifests are manifestations of

---

27 See e.g. the 40-second video explainer from 2023, 'How Earth REALLY moves through space' (youtube.com/watch?v=WwxhBirHkcQ), with the voice over concluding: "So if you think about it, Earth is not only our planet, but it's also kind of a spaceship".

28 Even if the Pentagon is still at pains to deny any knowledge of UAPs (UFOs) being of extraterrestrial origin, a distinctive force field can be seen around the objects in the videos captured by US Navy fighter jets and released by the Pentagon in 2020.

this Great Supreme Intelligence. They will not harm any form, as we do, because they feel that if they harm the form, they harm the *very power* of a Supreme Being that manifested through that form and makes that form possible. This is another Law that they obey.

They respect each other. We on Earth make fun of the pick-and-shovel man. If I happen to be a great artist, acknowledged throughout the world, I am a famous man. The poor pick-and-shovel man *has not* been acknowledged by anybody. He is doing the worst kind or lowest type of a job, so people look down on him. They don't do that on other planets, and neither should we do it here. For if it were not for this pick-and-shovel man digging the minerals out of the earth from which the paints are made, my artistic talents wouldn't do me any good because I would have nothing to work with. Or if I paint the murals on the walls, it wouldn't do me any good until he digs the foundation for that wall to stand on. In other words, it takes all kinds of people, all kinds of talents which have been given to all kinds of forms for different purposes, to create a whole. As a unit they work together and make the whole thing possible.

This they recognize. As a result, they have no caste system or conflict as we have. No one wants to outdo another – they are all interested in each other. Serving one another in the best way they know, as they would like to be served themselves, is their big advancement. They are not super-human beings. They have a long way to go. They are a few thousand years ahead of us and that is about all. Thank God we too can have that kind of a future. That is one *sure* thing. No one can take that away from us. We may be slow getting there, but we are going to get there in spite of ourselves. Right now we are quite a stubborn group of people. We are like a man standing on a highway who won't budge. Nobody wants to get in trouble so no one hits him, and he is stubborn so he stands there. But a little breeze comes along sometimes and he moves in spite of himself. We, too, move in spite of ourselves. The best job that one can do today is to start utilizing the knowledge, gradually, patiently, that has been granted and has proved workable. These people are working it, and that is why they are coming our way. I cannot state these things in public, altogether, because it would be wrong; but I can tell you this much — *these people are here!*

I have a letter here that I read at the press conference[29] and also during the radio interview with Ross Mulholland.[30] I got it from England on April 29. It says, "Today I was told by an American aeronautics engineer that a scientist high up in the Radio Corporation of America told him that it is now known that there are 1200 people living in the United States who *were not born on this planet!*" When I was in New York recently I lectured to what they call the 'Four Hundred'.[31] I thought I would read this letter to that group because if anybody knew anything about it they might say something. Sure enough, after I read it a man in the back of the room said, "so that leaked out!" So there was a confirmation of what I had read. Then I took the liberty to go on and say that if one institution can pin-point 1200 people, then those people might be employed by that institution while twelve thousand or twelve million might be walking our streets. No one said anything to that, but after the lecture a reception was held and I found out that the man who spoke up is one of the men at the R.C.A.

There is much that is not known, but one thing is definite — there *is something* taking place. We have had two wars and the last one killed off a lot of people. Many people came here from Europe and many people have moved from place to place within our own country. The days have gone when families had from seven to sixteen children, and yet we have more people than we have ever had! Some time ago there was a statement in the *Los Angeles Times* to the effect that there were over ten million people in this world whom no one knows anything about or where they came from. You ask, "But how do they do it? They have to have social security and one thing or another."

---

29 As Adamski likely gave several press conferences during his lecture tour to promote *Inside the Space Ships*, we cannot be certain that he refers to his press conference with the ministers of Detroit here — see page 25 ff.

30 Ross Mulholland (d.1991) was a radio personality who hosted a morning show on Detroit's WWJ station until 1957.

31 An arbitrary, informal group of affluent influential New Yorkers, originating with a list of socialites that was first drawn up during New York's 'Gilded Age' of the late 19th century.

In the first place, many people cross national borders without even a passport and they get away with it. If our prophets of the past were able to foretell what would happen in the present (and it is happening) then we must admit one thing — that these people, who are further advanced than we are, must have known just when we would need their help. They could have been mingling with us for a long time trying to elevate us a little by dropping a little knowledge here and there for us to use and to grow by. They could have begun as far back as 150 years ago. By knowing that such conditions would finally come they could have dropped a family here, a family there, and become established, having children and grandchildren. They have been in constant contact and when new ones come, they just drop in on the established families. They are introduced as cousins or other relatives and the family helps them get settled. It would be no trouble at all. They have been preparing the way, and it would be no trouble at all for many of them to be here just on those grounds alone.

You may wonder why we don't meet them, but you might be meeting a lot of them every day, and not even know it! They are no different than you or I. For example, when I was autographing books at the May Company[32], in Los Angeles, a young lady and her mother came up and told me about something that had happened to them. They were standing at the intersection of 5th and Broadway, waiting for the light to change so they could cross the street when a strange man walked up to them and asked, "Ladies, may I help you?" They saw that he was a very good looking man and they received a very kind feeling from him, but they had no packages and there was nothing that required any help, so they were a little frightened by his statement. They couldn't understand it along with that strange feeling they got from him that you don't usually get from everybody. They became a little disturbed and frightened, and before they realized what they were doing they said, "No." So the man just walked away. After they got home and thought it over they decided to come and ask me what I thought about it. Well there is

---

32 A major department store that operated in Los Angeles from 1925-1986.

no question in my mind that he was one of the visitors. He probably spoke to them because he knew that they are very serious minded about this situation. They go to the desert often to watch for saucers and they pray almost daily that they will meet one of the visitors. When they did they didn't recognize him.

It is a matter of recognition. There is a story that you have probably heard about Jesus. It was rumored that He was coming down a certain street one day. A certain woman went to work early in the morning and scrubbed and cleaned her house, hoping that she might be honored by having the Master walk into her home and bless her with His presence. She scrubbed the front porch thoroughly and no sooner had she finished when a child who had been wallowing in the mud came up and got the porch dirty. She ran him off with a broom and cleaned up the mess. Next a dog came along and did the same thing. She ran it off and cleaned up again. Soon the Master came down the street but He passed by the house without stopping. The woman ran after Him and called to Him. But Jesus said to her, "I have been there two different times and each time I was chased away." You can never tell when it is going to be unless your inner self is in tune with that All-Inclusive Self. These people were not quite in tune and they missed a good opportunity. There are many cases I could tell about that would take hours. People say, "Oh, I'm not afraid of them. Not at all." Yet six couples went to the desert regularly every week-end for over a year (slept out in sleeping bags) hoping to get a contact. Finally one night it happened. A ship came down within six feet of them. One of the ladies caught sight of a beautiful face at the porthole and she screamed. If it had been an ugly face I could understand why she would scream, but this was a beautiful face. Had only she screamed, maybe it would have been all right, but when she screamed the others followed like a bunch of cattle. They ran like the dickens and the ship went away. At three o'clock in the morning they drove up to my home and told me what happened. As Art Linkletter says, "People are funny."[33] We are all funny.

---

33 Art Linkletter (1912-2010) was a radio and TV personality who hosted the show 'People are funny', that ran from 1942 to 1960.

All this is happening *today*, and if we could get the top religious leaders of this world to come half way and acknowledge what is happening, which is a fulfilment of prophecy, I assure you that within six months or so, you could enjoy the privilege of having one of these ladies or men sitting at your dinner table some weekend. But at the present time — NO! Everything that has been announced about them to date from the material side of life, as we call it, has been received on the hostile side. We complain about the government, etc., but we have no complaint coming. We are doing the wrong thing when we do that. The government is YOU. I have been in the Pentagon when news was released. For two days things run on an even keel, letters and wires come in on the nice side. Then the trouble starts. Panic! Panic! Panic! What can the officials do, let the panic go on? All they can do is discredit the thing, to stop that panic. It is up to you. It is up to all of us to get settled down. We must have a little bit more faith in the things that are to come. We must be *patient* in trying to understand them!

Here is another very important point. In the past few years many flying saucer groups have sprung up, pro and con, causing a cut-throat business that is far from the purpose for which the saucers are coming – far from their purpose! Myths, too, have built up like a web until the people can't even find out what the real truth is. It is amazing. So many are getting on the bandwagon, either for self-prestige or for money. I might as well tell you the truth. That is what is going on. It is another reason for the confusion. And no one of a decent mind likes it, nor do those who are coming our way to help us. People are very odd. A person in New York asked me, "George, you have tremendous power, do you ever get frightened?" I said, "Why should I get frightened? I don't even know that I have any power, because I don't intend to use it in the manner you speak of." Yes, I could high-hat the people.[34] I'm independent. If I have never been before, I am now. As I said before, I could just call on each person for one dollar and I'd be a rich man. But I can't take it with me. I am sixty-four years old and don't have too many more

---

34   I.e. act superior towards others.

years to go. None of us are going to stay here forever, I know that. I would be a fool, I'd be crazy to go out and peddle something that I, myself didn't believe just because I thought people were suckers. I lived before the saucers came so I don't have to make money on them to live. Now I am known throughout the world, either as a crackpot or a darned good fellow. I could really make use of that publicity, but what good would it do me? My conscience must go with me wherever I go. Even if I didn't believe in the hereafter form the standpoint of religion, I would have to believe in it from the standpoint of science. Science tells you that matter can be changed in form, from state to state, but the essence that makes up matter can never be destroyed. Common sense tells you then — that which governs matter and puts it into a form is Intelligence; if matter is indestructible in its true essence, then surely the Intelligence that governs it is equally indestructible, and must face itself someplace. There is a Law of Harmony that governs our planets so well that they don't collide with each other, or bite each other, or punch each other's noses as we do. Unless we, as individuals, comply with that Law, that Perfect Harmony, we will have to face that Law someday! I don't want that day of reckoning if I can help it! I may do something wrong ignorantly, no man is perfect and no men are saints to the same degree, but I will eliminate all that I can of imperfection. When I *know* that something might be wrong, I won't act on it.

There are so many who would stick their neck out, take chances saying, "I'll challenge this. I have tomorrow." How do you know you have tomorrow? We always have survived until 'tomorrow', but one day there will be no tomorrow, and then it will be too late! In the meantime, you don't have to deny yourself anything. You can, and should, be normal. When in Rome, do as the Romans do. People say, "Since you have had those contacts, met those wonderful people, how can you live *here* now?" Well, I have met wonderful people in New York, in Los Angeles, and now here in Detroit. I have lived the *conscious alertness* of them all. If I had not gone to New York or Los Angeles, but lived all the time in Detroit, and that was all I knew, I'd be conscious only of Detroit. Now I have added to my knowledge by knowing something about New York, Los Angeles and Detroit. That is an expansion by which you become alerted to many things. But you still can live a normal life. ONLY NORMALCY which is natural will survive. Fanaticism, extremities, will not. For Nature doesn't have any extremities. She accepts only what She IS, and that is all.

Questions and answers

Question: In one of your lectures you said that the people of Venus never saw the stars until they got out into space away from their planet.
Answer: That is right. They have what we call clouds around the planet the same as we had at one time. The Bible calls it the firmament.

Q: How did the Venusians find out their planet is in motion revolving around the sun?
A: That is quite simple. The overcast is quite far out and they get certain sun's rays coming through. It is just like the thin clouds we have. The clouds don't always stay in one position any more than our clouds do. There is a break here and there, and they see the sun every now and then.

Q: You say there are a lot of these people here among us on Earth. How do they do it?
A: Yes. I have already explained how easily that could be handled. But do you think even if the authorities knew about them they would let you know? They wouldn't. And they wouldn't prosecute them either. I have a case in mind which happened about three years ago. A man in Korea did much good in performing surgery. There was an article about him in *Life* magazine. He deserted both the Navy and the Army. He had done everything. They should have given him twenty years, at least. But he is still free. There is a reason behind it!

Q: What method do these people use to attain the higher state of awareness that they have.
A: I analyzed the whole thing during the lecture, from Feeling on I gave you all the senses. I don't know of any more I can say that will give you a method.

Q: Well, for instance, we use different methods in our religions, etc. Do they also have different methods?
A: They do not! They have no caste system of any kind. All separate methods are caste systems.

Q: No, I don't mean caste systems.
A: But it *is* a caste system as soon as you begin to divide anything. It is not supposed to be divided. It is supposed to be even. Caste system doesn't mean a colored man over there and a white man over here especially. In India they have a caste system in the labor department, a separation of different levels.

Q: But how did they obtain the kind of state of awareness that they have now?
A: I just lectured on that. I showed you the five senses, told you which one is the Master Character that operates them, why the mortal mind was born, how it has conformed and what it does. I can't say any more. I have already explained it in detail. If you understand it right, you can go on and study and never have another question. (Mrs Marxer: It is a matter of attunement, in other words.)

Q: What is the medium of exchange that they use?
A: There is no medium of exchange as we understand it. It is more like a barter or trade system. All share equally the products of labor, with no coin.

Q: Does Father Baker claim that he is from another planet?[35]
A: No, he didn't say that. He said he didn't believe Adam was born here but was brought here from another planet.

Q: Can the space ships come over our radar nets without detection?
A: Yes, that has been done, but most of the time they are detected.

Q: Are these space people here for a particular purpose?
A: Yes, they are. Jesus said, "You are your brothers' keeper." We are

---

35 See also page 54.

brothers regardless of whether we live in Germany or the United States. We are human and acknowledge the same Creator. The same is true in reference to planets. I think they took it upon themselves to offer their help if we are willing to accept it. They have seen the mess we are in.

Q: Can these people go back to their own planet after they have accomplished what they came here to do?
A: Yes. The ones who gave me so much information have gone back.

Q: Have you had any more meetings with the space people since you were here before? If so, how many?
A: I have had three meetings. The third one was on April 25, just before my book went to the publishers.

Q: Have you had any contacts since then and if so, where?
A: Yes, one. It was in New York.

Q: Would you care to tell how it came about?
A: No.

Q: Is this Character within us what Christ referred to when He said to Nicodemus, "Unless you are born of the Spirit, you will not see the Kingdom of Heaven?"
A: That is right! He also said this, "The natural man knows the way of the Spirit. The unnatural man knows not the way of the Spirit." It is the same.

Q: With your experiences thus far, would you care to comment on the prophecy yet to be fulfilled, concerning the rapture of the church, the seven years of tribulation of Jacob, and the millennium?
A: If the churches don't wake up in time, they will face that condition by 1970. I will say more on that tomorrow night when I speak on world conditions.[36]

---

36 See the next lecture, 'The World of Tomorrow', page 79.

Q: Do the space people practise individualism?
A: Yes, the individual as [in] the identity of the individual, but not personality. There is a difference between the two.[37]

Q: Is there more than one race of people on these other planets? Is so, do they inter-marry and create other races?
A: All planets are made up very much like our own. They do not inter-marry to the degree of extremity, but they do not belittle those extremities either. They give them the same equal right as far as the social life of the planet is concerned.

Q: Where these people redeemed by Christ as we were?
A: That is a good question and it should be cleared up. The Catholic Church expressed it very well about three years ago with statements to the effect that it is quite possible to conceive that people on other planets could have started out in the right way. They committed no sin and have gone forward. We have committed sin and we have to work out of it. If they had not committed a sin, why would Christ need to sacrifice Himself for them? There would be no reason.[38]

Q: We are supposed to have been born with original sin. That includes the Universe.
A: Nothing of that kind was said either in the Bible or any other documents.

Q: It doesn't say anything in the Bible about the Universe. It says Man.
A: Yes, here! The Bible only talks about *here* and everything that

---

37 According to the Tibetan Master Djwhal Khul, "Two major ideas should be taught to the children of every country. They are: the value of the individual and the fact of the one humanity" — in other words, unity in diversity. See Alice A. Bailey (1954), *Education in the New Age*, p.47.

38 According to the Ageless Wisdom teaching, the 'sin' spoken of here should be understood as humanity's straying from the Path by losing sight of the oneness of all Life. Christ did not sacrifice Himself to wash away our sins, but Jesus sacrificed himself to illustrate the need to surrender the personal self, the ego, to the Higher Self, the Christ consciousness in the heart, that which Adamski referred to as the Master Character that operates through the senses of the personality.

transpired on Earth. It tells the history and development of this race. I can show you where the words Lord, Gods, and Angels come from and how each of the civilizations fell by the way. There were large numbers of ships that landed in various places in earlier civilizations. With no communication systems as we have today to get messages from one corner of the world to another, each group considered itself special because these ships came from the sky where Heaven is supposed to be. They began to worship the Visitors and anything that came from the sky was classified as Lord, God, or Angel.

Q: How do you expect all of the people to hear of this?
A: The Bible says that the awakening of the Christ consciousness will come, or that conscious men will become conscious of Christ's presence in the midst of them. As Jesus said, "Wherever there are two or three gathered in my name, there shall I be in the midst of them." Maybe that is what is really coming forth. I do not expect *too* much, but I do believe that the spiritual leaders of the people of the world are totally responsible for anything that might happen from now on. They have taken the job on their shoulders. The world is in a bad mess today. We know that many nations are not Christian nations but France, Poland, Italy, Germany and Britain are Christian in name, as we are, and we cannot deny that both wars were Christian wars. Something is wrong with our understanding of Jesus' teachings. He said to Peter, "If you live by the sword, by the sword you shall also die." That is what we have done, and it means that we have never believed His teachings – for that which a man believes, *he lives!*

Q: How can the masses be expected to believe?
A: The revelations will come just as soon as a group of people accept it. All of the Christian doctrines state that it will be the minority, not the majority that will believe. So you can't bank on the majority.

Q: If it is not going to be the majority then why do you say that the visitors will not come down until we get all the people to believe?

A: Because we don't even have a minority now.[39]

Q: You have a lot bigger minority now than when Christianity started out, sir.
A: Yes, we do. But we have a lot more people now, too, than when Christianity started. It shows, too, the narrowness on the part of our professed teachers who question what is happening today. That is why we are in a mess. The Bible says that in those latter days, the Son of Man will come down from the sky, or Heaven, to Earth and that all the yellow and colored races, throughout the world will rise and demand the rights that the white man has enjoyed. Today you have the greatest trouble in Asia.[40]

Q: Can a person be contacted by being impressed to write something?
A: We are not talking in those fields at all now.
(Ed. note: The person who asked this question said that she was not referring to automatic writing, but inspiration. Mr. Adamski says many people have been impressed to take a certain line of action.)

Q: Can you explain the bright lights in some of the craters and the letter H that have been seen many times on the face of the moon by amateur astronomers?
A: The bright lights on the moon are peaks on the mountains. They are there all the time. But when you find bright lights in the bottoms of the craters one day, and the next day you see them moving in and out, that is something else again.

Q: Is it known if any woman has had contact with space people?
A: Last year two Norwegian women had a direct contact. It was well publicized in the United States but not as truthfully as it happened. Some editors in Norway wrote to me and asked how close it was to mine. The same thing happened to them as happened to me. There have been other women contacted also. Altogether there have been

---

39 See also pages 34 and 48.
40 See also page 27, note 6, and page 79.

about 1500 contacts throughout the world to date — both men and women.[41]

Q: Was there any message or significance in the [1955 motion] picture, 'This Island Earth'?
A: I couldn't say. I didn't see the picture. But the picture *The Day the Earth Stood Still* was significant. I have a French paper that says the picture was 95% correct and that it really happened in Juneau, Alaska, in the early part of 1948 when the first contact with a government official was made.[42]

Q: Do you think that [fellow contactee] Buck Nelson is sincere?
A: I have never met Mr. Nelson so I can't say. I have no right to judge from rumors and I have never talked to him personally.[43]

Q: In his lecture, Mr. Nelson said he and the visitors slept during their trips from one planet to another. I should think a person would be too excited to want to sleep at a time like that.
A: I know what you mean. If I were awake and the world was coming to an end right now, I'd be the last one to go off of it, if I could help it, because I would want to see the last act.

Q: Have these people progressed since the beginning of time to an actual stage where they are in attunement with God more than we are?
A: There is really no beginning of time, but we use that as a measuring stick to convey thoughts to each other. They have progressed beyond us, yes. But I know of no person today, here or anywhere

---

41 Two notable early examples of women contactees who wrote about their experiences are Margit Mustapa, who emigrated from Finland to the USA, and Elizabeth Klarer from South Africa.

42 Robbie Graham's suggestion (in *Silver Screen Saucers*, p.140) that Adamski's account in *Inside the Space Ships* might have been inspired by *The Day the Earth Stood Still*, which premiered in 1951, ignores the fact that Adamski had already described highly evolved space beings giving him the same message during his out-of-body experiences in *Pioneers of Space*, published in 1949. See also Aartsen (ed., 2022), op cit.

43 See also page 40, note 22.

in this world, who is not constantly in contact with God. According to the Bible when God created a man on this earth, He commanded the Spirits to gather the dust of the earth and bring forth man — the same as a sculptor carving one out of clay. After He looked upon it He liked the image which must have been of His Thought or what He had expected to come forth. Then He breathed the Breath of Life into the nostrils and it became a living soul known as Man.[44]

Show me a man or woman, whether he is aware of it or not, who can live more than four minutes in the absence of the air he breathes. No man sells it to us — it is freely given. Should he not breathe, no man would be considered as a living being no matter how good a body he has. As I have said, the visitors respect every form so much that they will not hurt it, because if they did they would be hurting, or belittling That which the form represents. The form in general, and man especially, represents the Deity, according to our own teachings, since He created man in His image and His likeness.

Q: Are the visitors angels compared to us?
A: Compared to us they would be angels, but not as we define Angels.

Q: Do the space people advocate that Adam and Eve were brought here from another planet?
A: I haven't asked them. But my first contact informed me that he had lived here on earth a thousand years ago. Methuselah lived 999 years on this Earth. At that time, if you remember correctly, there was a firmament over this whole Earth. If you study your Bible correctly you will find that when that firmament burned away the span of life also started to go down. And with the best of scientific and medical advancement we can't control some of the things that have come up in the form of diseases, even today. There is a good reason behind it.

---

44 For an esoteric interpretation of this metaphor, see e.g. H.P. Blavatsky (1888), *The Secret Doctrine*, Vol.II, Anthropogenesis.

Q: (The question was not discernible on the tape.)
A: I understand the question. Shafts of light can be seen sometimes in total darkness, and the shaft will appear not too luminous but will be a flash before your eyes, going across very fast. They are magnetic beams, concentrated at the time, that are testing the conditions of our own Earth. In New York I was given a very good article on magnetic influence taking place throughout the world today. There is much to be said about what is taking place on the Earth, and there is a big thing that is the cause of the present conditions that cannot be blamed on the atomic bomb alone.

(Ed. note: Mr. Adamski has explained in other lectures that one of the main reasons for the visitors coming is the shift in the magnetic poles of this planet.[45])

---

45 Esotericist and futurologist Benjamin Creme said in 1998 that the shifting of the poles was prevented by the Space Brothers. See Creme (2001), *The Great Approach – New Light and Life for Humanity*, p.130. On May 7, 2024 a BBC Science Focus report confirmed: "Earth's magnetic field is overdue a flip" (see: <www.sciencefocus.com/planet-earth/earth-magnetic-field>).

The World of Tomorrow

Talk by George Adamski

Detroit Institute of Arts
September 20, 1955

I thought I would take up the question tonight in reference to what we might expect in years to come and why we are in the condition in which we find ourselves today. Very few people realize just what has been taking place. We have been moving so fast, in so many ways, that we overlook many things and cannot quite place ourselves at the moment as to why all these things are taking place as they do, including 'flying saucers' among many other things.

In the first place, we have prophecies that we have overlooked — Mother Shipton[1], Nostradamus, the Bible, and many others, and I might say right here that those prophecies are actually coming true, if we look at them in the right way. For example, it states in our own Bible that in the latter days (as we might call it at the moment) that when these things will be happening — like "signs in the sky and war and rumors of war" — we will have come to an end of a cycle, or as some people call it, a "dispensation". These things are taking place right at the very moment. At the same time, there is a statement made also that the yellow races everywhere will be rising and demanding the rights that the white man has enjoyed all these ages. We have such trouble today in Asia.[2]

So there's your fulfillment right there to really know why the disturbed conditions in this world. We are moving, moving slowly, sometimes a little fast, other times slowing up, but we are moving forward. Go back to the time of 1945 (or even before 1945) since the war ended; our own government, as well as every government

---

1   Born Ursula Soothtale (or Sontheil, c.1488-1561), Mother Shipton was an English soothsayer and prophetess.
2   See also page 27, note 6; and page 75.

in the world, is not the same government as it was. If you look back even two years, you will find a tremendous change has taken place.

We find, if we look back, that science especially is moving faster than any time in the history of our civilization. At one time, science was actually ignored. Many great men and minds have died by the wayside with ideas that could have put us forth probably one hundred years farther than what we are. But they were ignored. A scientist may conceive ideas, but he may not have the means to back them up. The people didn't back them op — they didn't even think the ideas worthwhile — they were afraid to move forward even if they saw the idea. As a result, we have not moved too fast.

But since the war (a more or less scientific type of war, where scientific instruments were used) the governments all over the world have backed science up. In the last ten years they have moved further than they have moved in the last hundred years — and they are moving so fast that if we continue as we do today, no one can say just what this nation or this whole world will be like, say by 1970. There are many things coming forth.

Just in New York, I was talking at the offices of the National Broadcasting Company. We were talking about the many things that are transpiring today. We find that even right now they are already developing instruments in surgery where the knife (in operating) is no longer going to be used in the manner it has been, but 'high frequency'. Things like that are taking place.

The president of Lear Company of Los Angeles made a statement not so long ago that one of these days, and probably long before we actually will have a space ship of our own going into outer space, that we will go into a booth, something like a phone booth, with baggage and all, and ask for the prices to New York from Los Angeles. They will tell you the price, you will deposit the money (like you do in the telephone box) and someone, somewhere, will push a button — and in less than a split second you will be in New York. This sounds impossible, but nevertheless those are possibilities that we are facing today. They are coming gradually for man has only scratched the surface of electronics — and as he goes along, he will discover many other things.

You ladies, one of these days, will not have to be buying brooms.

Your houses will probably be wired with magnetic lines or positive force around your floor, where your dust would be attracted. Since all particles are negative, the positive line would attract them like today a magnet attracts dusts of iron.[3]

All those things are coming forth. It's only a matter of time, and I would say by 1960, if things go right, and we do not have a global war of an atomic nature, which would have a tendency or actual potential of destroying this civilization, that we should go forward. We should go to such a civilization as has never been known on this Earth before — a lot further than many others you have probably read about — Atlantis, Lemuria, and other civilizations that have advanced far. I should say that we will advance a lot further, if we ourselves today can trust science. When I say 'science', I don't mean all men are scientists because they are working in a scientific factory. I mean major science, science that works in the laboratory, that actually works with nature, not independent of nature.

Look to nature for discoveries, for we must admit that nature has given man nearly everything he has today. Even Edison, many times, when he got puzzled in the laboratory, would give up the whole idea and go up in the park some place and smoke a pipe. While he was free of the thought he was working on, suddenly an idea would be impressed upon his mind — and he would go to his laboratory and finish his job.

Man must look to nature. He is a by-product of nature (we can say it that way) — she is his Mother and can give him any answer he wants, providing he goes to her in the right way and actually listens to what he is supposed to be listening to, instead of his own mind

---

3   In his 1964 article 'The Space People' Adamski describes life on Venus: "As an example, They have an attractor that gathers all particles of dust from their homes; the dust is not released outside but is deposited in containers for that purpose. The dust is gathered from these containers and taken to a central plant, where it is processed to extract the minerals from the particles, *for they do not waste anything*." See Aartsen (2010), *George Adamski – A Herald for the Space Brothers*, p.113. The fact that he mentions this technology in his talk in September 1955 suggests that he had already witnessed it on one of his trips in space. Interestingly, in 2023 a scientific paper was published that discussed the removal of dust from solar panels using a weak electric field. See <doi.org/10.1016/j.rser.2023.113471>.

rattling, sometimes wild, not finding any answers to his problems.

We will find that probably by 1970 we will also have automobiles as we have today, but they will not have any wheels. They will not run on gasoline as ours do today. Take Los Angeles — it is in a terrible state; New York is coming along the same way, and many other cities. The more cars we have, the more exhaust we will have, and much of that fuel is not burned — smog is created, which is not good for human beings anywhere. This has become quite a problem, and especially in Los Angeles, as you have probably read. It is not very pleasant.

So these new things must come forth if this civilization is going to survive in a good healthy state. We will have to adopt other means by which we can propel ourselves from place to place. That next step will be to harness the very power that you have been reading that the flying saucers or spacecraft use. These people (from other planets) do not use fuel like we use — and they are moving through space. We will have this power harnessed and probably much earlier than we realize. We will have automobiles and everything else propelled by this power. This power is tremendous — far greater than you realize — and it is inexhaustible.[4]

This world has been in existence for ages and ages, millions upon millions of years. Yet, there were other bodies, other worlds in existence prior to this world, and they keep going. By what power? When we stop to think for a moment, we begin to realize that some great power is really propelling these bodies through space.

For instance, our own world is moving at the rate of 162 miles per second on the orbit side of the Sun, while it moves nearly 19 miles per second on the 24-hour basis. We find that it makes nearly 600 million miles per year — and we do not know anything about it. (We don't even know it has moved an inch.) Our earth is 25,000 miles around. That's quite a large sized body to be moved through

---

4   It is a public secret that over, say, the past century efficient and clean alternative energy sources have been discovered or developed, which were then acquired and shelved by the fossil fuel industry. Had our economic system not been ceded to market forces but made to serve all of humanity equally, such alternative energy sources could have transformed our world in the time span indicated by Adamski here.

space at that speed. Then we find Jupiter out there, actually eleven times bigger than our own world. In fact, if it was cut up into our own size, it would make eleven of our worlds. Then, we find many other bodies that are far larger than that, and are all moving just like toys through space. We never give much thought to this. Yet, there they are — no one is pushing them, no 'jet engines' on them, no 'wings' — but there they are floating through space.

We have a tendency in this world to think that nothing is really happening because we don't feel any movement. The ancients thought there was a prop holding this Earth up someplace, or strings holding it from above. Yet, all you have to do is to look out into space. Other planets are moving across the heavens as well and there is nothing holding them up. They are actually floating in a sea of power. That power can be harnessed — has been harnessed — by those of other planets. Why cannot it be harnessed by our own scientists? They will harness it; they are already working along that line.

In fact, if you go back to about 1928, you find Lindbergh[5] and many others were involved in the particular plan of a young man by the name of Hendershot[6] who was working on a certain generator. The generator was being devised under the supervision of the military. This man Hendershot himself was knocked so badly by this power that he spent some time at the Bellevue Hospital.

So it is not really a mystery entirely. The mystery is how to develop to a stage where we can run the whole world with it — to run anything that requires power.

We are puzzled by many things. We are puzzled how the saucers 'fly'. Yet, if we look at the situation correctly, we must admit at we ourselves as a world are nothing but a space ship moving at that rate of speed. None of us know of this movement.

These people have harnessed that power; utilize the same law by

---

5 In 1927 Charles Lindbergh (1902-1974) made the first non-stop flight between New York and London.

6 As the inventor of the 'fuelless motor', Lester Hendershot (1899-1960) made headlines in 1928 when the *New York Times* wrote in its edition of 28 February: 'Fuelless Motor Impresses Experts'. See <www.rexresearch.com/stuff/stuff11/hendershot_book.pdf>. (The original transcript has 'Hendershaw', which was probably misheard from the tape recording; see also the Introduction, page 5.)

which they operate their space ships which are 'man-made planets', and they are puzzling to us because we have failed to look at our own (planet), from which we could learn just what is taking place.

We are also coming to the stage in development (and this may be disastrous to certain groups), when we will be dealing with this force in such a manner that no human being will have to suffer from disease. That time is not too far off, either. For instance, medical science has advanced a long way, done wonders in many things. Yet, with all their advancement today, we find there are many new diseases coming up with which they cannot cope.

Now, we find a great disturbance in the world of the human mind. Well, a human being is a by-product of nature (let us put it that way). Nature, the Mother Earth, has given him a body. That body is only transformed earth into flesh and blood and bones. It goes back there. You might as well face it. Well, naturally, if the Mother Earth, herself, gets a little shaky, let us say, you are going to be feeling it yourself. You're related to it in that manner. Well, the Mother Earth *is shaky*, you might say, at this time.

Just how far she's going to go with it is anybody's guess. No one really knows. But we do know that there's something going on in this world and we do know that this year we had quite a number of bad conditions produced by nature. Millions of dollars lost, disasters caused by hurricanes; hot weather in California (in places) were it was not known before.

A lot of people have a tendency to blame this on the atom bomb. Let me say to you the atom bomb might have had a little to do with it, but it didn't do all that. It couldn't. It's impossible for it to bring such a disturbance as that. Because you might say the lightning formed is equivalent to that and is not disturbing conditions. But what is really happening, might be said, is this: most of you have read that prior to the war, Admiral Byrd went to Little America.[7]

---

7 Admiral Richard E. Byrd (1888-1957) was an American naval officer and a polar explorer who established the first Little America exploration base in Antarctica in 1929. His claim to be the first to reach the North Pole by air in 1926 was later disputed. In 1946 Admiral Byrd was put in charge of the first post-war scientific Antarctic expedition. Known as Operation Highjump, this expedition has been widely rumoured to have been in search of a secret Nazi base.

When he came back, he told us there was nothing but ice and snow — solid everywhere. Yet, after the war had ended, he went to Little America again and came back with a different kind of story. What was that? He said that the ice and snow was thawing, melting very fast and that rivers and lakes were forming, and even vegetation was beginning to show here and there.[8] We must admit again that to bring conditions like that about in that part of the world, some change had to take place to produce that climatic condition which did not exist there before.

You see, since the Earth itself is moving on the side, what they call shifting off its axis, then you and I and everyone is going to be disturbed, whether we know what is disturbing us or not.[9] Unless we know what is taking place, we'll be guessing at many things and often blaming many things for our uneasy feelings. We are, you might say, a sensitive instrument that is able to register and speak what we feel.

How far all this will go, no one can tell you. However, the scientists that are good are on the job, watching with the instruments they have, carefully checking to see what is really happening. So far, no danger is showing, but at the same time, the climatic conditions like we have had this summer could easily have been brought about by a slight shift of the Earth that could produce a current to cause such storms as we have been having. It has done that before. We have a cold condition in one section and suddenly it begins to get warm — it is going to produce a terrific storm or vortex or whirlwinds that will travel any distance.

---

8   The only reference that can be found to this effect is to early 1950s reports in which paranormal writer and publisher Ray Palmer (editor of *Fate* magazine, among others) hinted that Admiral Byrd had flown beyond the North Pole and reported seeing mountains, forests and other vegetation instead of ice and snow. Since the 1970s a 'missing diary' of Admiral Byrd's has been circulating, which allegedly describes his flight from the Arctic Base camp to the North Pole on 19 February 1947 when, incredibly, the Admiral flies into a huge cavern (the 'inner Earth'). Here he meets with someone he refers to as 'the Master' of a highly evolved civilization who asks him to warn the 'surface world' of the dangers of nuclear warfare. See e.g. Geoff Douglas (comp., 2017), *Admiral Richard E. Byrd's Missing Diary*.

9   See also page 78, note 45.

Now we also have the space ships that are coming. Why are they coming? They are not going to conquer you and me or impose any religion upon us or any kind of ideas upon us. They will share their knowledge with us if we care to have it, but they are not going to force it. Their main observation is, really, the same shift of our own Earth. It's not only our own Earth but the whole system that is going through a change which is a cycle that is coming to an end and another will take its place. From there on, she'll ride on even keel again.

We don't know what it is going to bring us, as I stated before, but we have had such conditions in times gone. Biblical history has recorded some of them. Some of them we have no record of, because history was not written that early and if it was the civilization that wrote it went down and the history with it. The library of Alexandria could have had probably much of that history but it was burned by fanatics. So we can only go back on the history of our biblical nature and see that things have taken place like this on Earth at one time, like Noah's flood, for instance. That was a natural catastrophe.

Yet, we are also in a position to bring in human catastrophe upon ourselves. We are not careful, not patient enough to wait and let things work out by themselves as they will. We can through impatience bring a conflict of atomic warfare that would finally annihilate us all. But, by keeping your minds open — you don't have to swallow everything that anybody tells you. You'd be foolish if you did. But you have got a mind of your own, all you have to do is use it. When you use it, you'll get an understanding of yourself. In that way, you can govern yourself very well and you can be ready for what might come. Any great advancement — you will fit right into it; any changes — you will fit into them. That's the only way you can. These are the only people that will fit into these times.

Remember, too, that the masses as a whole have always been against the few. Always have been — you can read history. People have always been afraid to change. Yet change is something that is forced by nature herself, as is taking place today. Some are afraid to speak because of loss of job; others because of loss of prestige or friendship; others won't speak out of fear of total criticism by a humanity which might not understand them. As far as history goes, we find that all of our great men and women of scientific or philosophical nature have been crucified, condemned, and even burned at the stake in earlier days because they were not understood, and only because they saw things to come. Here we have those things they saw at that time! It is only now that science has 'freedom', you might say, to go ahead to better humanity.

When I say 'science' I mean true science, on the grounds that a true scientist doesn't care what your faith may be, what your color may be, what your education is. When he finds something that is beneficial to mankind, he hands it over to the whole world. *He* is a true scientist. We are in that stage today and unless the faiths of our world wake up to this moment, they also will be just a matter of history.

If you could see the letters that I receive. I got a letter (from home) today, telling me that last week over 3,500 letters came in, and most of them are from young people 15 to 30 years of age. They are all asking the questions that we are talking about tonight. We, the older people, must eventually make way for them. Unless our faiths go along with the movement of the day, these youngsters will probably turn away from the doors of the churches.

We have already started a program that is far more amazing and holds more future for us than anything that has been ever undertaken on this planet before. That is when Eisenhower signed a Bill for the first satellite to go out. That is the beginning of venturing into space, pioneering, by ourselves. He is not the only one. Notice that the Four Great Powers of the world at the Geneva Conference, made the statement simultaneously, after he signed the Bill. So it is a world movement, not one nation. This is the tendency today, and has been for some time. Take Wendell Willkie's *One World*[10] — the United Nations has promise of that result and are pushing that same way. There is something transpiring in this world that we never dreamed would take place in our time, but it is taking place — the tendency toward a United World.

---

10 Wendell L. Willkie (1892-1944) was an American lawyer and liberal Republican whose book, published in 1943, advocated an end to colonialism, world federalism, and equality for non-whites in the USA.

Why not? If we do admit there is a great power which has put us here and has also created this world? I believe, myself, that this power meant for all that were placed upon this planet to be as a family, not as strangers, and go where they wish to go upon this great ball of dirt. Now, if that was in the beginning, the chances are that the issue is coming up now that the fulfillment will take place.

We are facing this condition today and must look up to it, have an open mind; for the first satellite going out there is not going to be the last, I assure you. There will be others!

Before I left California, the Convair System — I know Mr. McFarlin of their experimental department quite well — made a statement that if all goes right, within 18 months we will have a ship that will move from New York to England in 90 minutes![11]

The general public does not really realize just what is going on. True, we might say that we are in a state of war because we have not signed peace, and things are moving because of the necessity in that line. But don't forget, during such a research, other things are found beneficial to peace-time conditions. Much of that has been found already, that could be utilized for the good of humanity,

It is not surprising for Convair to come out with a statement like that. Besides, they came out with another, i.e. that only in a matter of a short time, two or three years, we will have a space craft going out into space — probably Venus or Mars.

I have an article right here published by CalTech, Pasadena — the group that controls the 100-inch telescope at Mt. Wilson and the 200-inch telescope at Mt. Palomar. Dr. Hubble[12] — I've known him well before he passed away — told us a couple of years ago, at a lecture in Philadelphia, that the 100-inch telescope alone had uncovered between one to three sextillion stars. And all are not stars as we call them, If you look into the heavens, you will notice that some do not blink; others do. Those that do not blink are

---

11 In fact, the fastest reported journey from New York to London was a US Air Force flight in 1974, that took one hour and 54 minutes.

12 Edwin Hubble (1889-1953) was an American astronomer who was instrumental in establishing extragalactic astronomy and observational cosmology. The Hubble Space Telescope launched in 1990 was named in his honour.

planets. Those that do blink are suns like our own. He said that the Earth is duplicated, probably, many, many times out there with the same climate, same air, same everything. I have that document.

So you see, we will not be aiming at any 'dead spot', as has been thought at first, but for some spot that some life is on. About nine months ago I made a statement which I made before and made emphatic, that I had not backed on at all, for it was no speculated thought — that there is air beyond our atmosphere. We've been taught that there wasn't, that it [i.e. space] was a vacuum. Yet, when the satellite was announced, what was the answer? They said that it (the satellite) will stay up in the air maybe two days at the most, then it will wear itself out by friction. It will buck the air that's there, which is light air, not as heavy as here, and thereby disintegrate.

We have to use a little common sense here. We know that Wolf Star 359 is eight light years away from us.[13] Don't misunderstand the light year question. A lot of people have an idea that light years exist between our planets. They don't. Same mileage you have on the speedometer in your car. It's only between systems that light years enter. Yet, we've been getting the code system from that body, known as Wolf Star 359, for the last seven years. What has been deciphered, I don't know — they're not releasing the information. But something has been deciphered and was recognized as intelligently sent. That's why an instrument was set up to catch it. Had it been jumbled, they would not have bothered with it. Now, to get a message and code system coming from such a great distance, anyone that's got any common sense must admit there must be something in space on which this message arrives. It's got to have a carrier.

We are only beginning to learn now — there were nothing but theories. Our instruments were not good enough to prove a lot of things to us. So we speculated on them. All they were, were theories. As we progress, in the field of science, we find that we develop better instruments. Just the other day I read an article where the present spectroscope is obsolete. We have a better one

---

13 At 7.86 light years distance Wolf 359, a red dwarf, is the fifth-nearest star to the Sun, located in the constellation Leo. Internet searches did not produce any reference to radio signals or fast radio bursts detected from Wolf 359 in the public domain.

now, one that will prove more truthful. [Ed. note: A spectroscope is a scientific instrument composed essentially of a prism and slit, used in astronomy to examine the spectra of solar light — separating rays into their prismatic colors so as to determine the substance.]

I have seen a T.V. program while I was in Los Angeles, where an atomic scientist was talking about the same thing, the spectroscope — that it was completely false except that it could be used on material right here, but not in outer space. Yet, we based a lot of our information on the spectroscope and figured we were right. On stage, the scientist showed a bowl, flat and loaded with water, and he let the public look through it to the other side, to see what the object on the other side of the bowl looked like. Much confusion. Nothing was outlined perfectly. That's what he said then and that's what the spectrum brings to us — because we go through 'dry' water, two hundred miles of it, which we call atmosphere. So we cannot get the exact truth of the chemicals.

Besides, here is another thing — judging those planets as to composition, climatic conditions and all upon them – science has admitted in the field of astronomy that space is full of space debris. All right, that debris can be made up of particles of dust, gases of various kinds. All these are going to register on the spectroscope long before the target is actually hit. If we do not know the interference that exists between us and that target, that other planet, whereby we could deduct the interference to the exact percentage, .how a.re we ever going to know what the truth is on that planet?

Yet, we are moving in that direction today. Thanks to electronics we are working to where the electronic system will finally be developed to such an extent that we'll be able to use it like a stick, extended, inch by inch — measure every inch of it (space) and then hit the target and deduce the percentages of interference and have the answer, even if we never go out with a space craft. Yet we will go out with a space craft much sooner than you realize. Space craft have been on drawing boards in airplane firms for some time.

I was talking to [Hermann] Oberth[14], one of the greatest scientists

---

14 See page 37, note 18.

in the world, as some people call him, while I was in Buffalo, New York. We talked quite a bit about these things. A space platform, such as we are planning, or other nations are planning, will serve us as a stepping stone. But it will not be the solution. Our solution will have to be something better than that. Besides, a space platform, if it goes out into space where there would be friction encountered, will wear itself out also, unless that space platform has a force-field around it, protected such as the Earth is protected by a force-field which we call atmosphere. And unless we get it to a balance, where the magnetic pull is both ways, like taking two magnets of equal strength and suspending something between them — the space platform will disintegrate. But even then, we wouldn't know if it would disintegrate or not. There is only one true answer to the space platform, that it may stand up for years to come, as the Earth does, and that is to produce the same condition around it, as the Earth has around itself.

We have been making fun at flying saucers, yet it is amazing how much we have already learned from them. Without them, we probably would not have been thinking in these terms today. They have not only awakened our minds to the potentials ahead of us, not only to the potentials of other human beings like ourselves, living on another body there, floating through space as we are — but they taught us what to look for in order to do the same thing. They have taught us much more than has been written down, or given to the public in general.

In all the years that they have been passing, no one has been hurt and, naturally, we must admit that the space craft of this type — that our or any other jets cannot catch up with — could do a lot of damage if they so wanted. Nobody can retaliate against them. But they have done nothing like that. It's not their purpose.[15] Their purpose is, again, as I go back to the thought — this whole system is making a slight change. You have two bodies in relationship to each other in that manner for thousands of years, suddenly one of them tilts and the relationship changes — the other will know it.

---

15 It should be noted that stories of 'alien abduction' did not appear before about a decade had passed of accounts of contacts with benevolent visitors only. See also Grant Cameron's comment on page 2.

As we have good instruments able to register earthquakes at 8,000 miles and further, we have just as good instruments to register tilts, ourselves. Scientists are using them today, watching the shifts of the Earth. These people being that much further ahead, proving to us that they are since they are traveling through space, must be even further ahead on such instruments and have detected that changes are occurring and began to move and see just what is happening in the system. For they too will probably be affected to some degree by these certain changes. They must be, for this system is like anything else — everything within it must be balanced or it cannot work. You knock a spoke out of a wheel, run it, and you wreck it unless you replace it. Think of our own system and planets here, even the slightest change in the air would bring about different conditions and would change conditions in general. That is one reason they are coming — which is quite scientific — and only as observers, we are learning much. A lot more than the public realizes.

I have an article written in France saying that the first satellite going out (further than the one just going out as a test) will carry 'flying saucer equipment' to help it along. A lot of people ask if the flying saucers have landed or have they not. Well, where did we know about this 'flying saucer equipment'? This has been published not in our but in the French papers, and they seem to know more about what we are doing than we ourselves! There is so much of this — naturally, a lot of it must be secretive. As I stated, the world is still at war, no peace has been signed. Any moment, things might happen and you have to guard against those moments. So some of the things we develop, we must keep secret. Not that we do not want the public to know, not that the public is not entitled to know it — but it must be kept secret. When the time comes that all is well, then these things will be known.

I have talked to a renowned man from General Electric. He said, "George, if we could put out the stuff we have already developed and put it into operation and let the public come and see it, it would be so fantastic that they wouldn't believe what they were seeing to be true." That's how far we have gone.[16]

Yes, indeed. The T.V. and such few things as we can enjoy in our homes today are very minor and quite obsolete — right today — and they are quite new to us. In the future, as we advance, T.V. will not be the T.V. that carries a picture from a few miles away, but we will get them not only from the planets in our own system, but also from far outer-space. They will do even more than that. You yourself will be able to communicate (no different than you do on the telephone today) with beings on other planets. Anybody can learn any language. We have people coming from foreign countries who learn our language quite well in a short time. Today, these people coming our way (from other planets) learn our language — how? They tune in on our radio and T.V. and learn in that way. It is no longer a problem. It calls for a little time, that is all.

We will find that our own cooking, even the raising of food will be done electronically. On these ships they do have that. They have green vegetation by the day. We are now beginning to realize for the first time that the same force that propels our Earth, as it does billions of planets in outer space, also produces our food, produces life through the process of breeding which you and I have to depend upon. In other words, we are getting at the source of all things. Once knowing how to use this knowledge, nothing will be impossible. All things will be made quite easy. Man will live as long as he wants without knowing age.

When you release humankind of this world from its strait-jacket of tension — the tension it finds itself in the day-by-day struggle for a living in the manner that it is all set up today — when you remove that, you have nearly removed all the causes of age, sickness, and possible death.[17]

---

16 On August 21, 2024 Harald Malmgrem, who served as senior advisor under presidents John F. Kennedy, Lyndon Johnson, Richard Nixon and Gerald Ford, made the news with his personal story that he was briefed on "otherworld technologies" by a top CIA official in the 1960s. See <www.news.com.au/technology/science/space/otherworld-technologies-former-presidential-aides-cia-claim/news-story/382a4345d70e89cf412442bced17b0f3>.

17 Article 25 of the Universal Declaration of Human Rights being the first step towards that blessed condition.

We are facing that type of a future, provided we do not become impatient and suddenly blow ourselves to bits by trying to grab from the other fellow. This is not worth the chance. When people get down to common sense and work out the problems that are to be worked out and let nature help them along, it's then we are going to consolidate and work as a unit toward the great good that is awaiting us.

All will have much time by the number of things being done with electronics — things they have to do themselves today. Much time to study, to develop the mind. Your mind is only about 1% in action at this time, with 99% to be developed. It must be admitted that a mind with only 1% of its potential developed, and has done what it has (even through error and pain) — what will it do when it has a chance to really develop as it should develop?! You will see a virtual heaven compared to what has been known. Look back to the cave-times. See what has been done up to this moment. At the beginning, man had so little to work with. He meant well but he did not have the instruments with which to work. What did he do? He actually had to dig a hole in the side of a hill to live in. Later, he knew how to cut timber and hew a house from it. Compare your own home to that of the past. Why, it's a palace, compared to one of, say 1900, in our own country. A few years from now what you call a palace today, you will look upon as a 'shack'!

That is how man progresses, not in one thing, but in everything. Let us use our eyes to see what is actually ahead of us. We may be disappointed at times. Nature has a role to play — we will find it hard to understand. Things will happen along the path. But remember there is always a little labor demanded from everyone, to get his reward at the end of the road.

Sometimes you wonder if these fiction writers have not something on the ball. Well, some of the stories are fantastic and quite contrary to nature, but there is also a decent foundation behind most of them.

I know a great astronomer, and what he knows about astronomy I cannot speak to you (of what he has told me) without jeopardizing his position, so he writes fiction in that same field to put it out that way. It's not the fault of the institutions, it is the fault of most people.

They fail to think. What they fail to learn by not thinking they will criticize the others who cannot stand the risk of being criticized. But if we ourselves, as humans, will make ourselves a little more liberal, at least walk in the middle of the road and not in the extremes, don't jump to conclusions, let time tell its story — and it will, always — then we will make it easier for these people, and then we will move a little faster because we can't be stubborn forever, that's for sure. If we have to move, let us move intelligently.

Also, in reference to the space people, who are coming our way — no greater evidence or greater statement has been made than that was made on July 17th at the Geneva Conference, when a publication came from there saying that there was a Bill introduced into the Conference to do something about or deal with the people of other worlds. It said nothing about their coming, it said more likely that they are here, mingling among us. That's the way it read. Now the Bill was right in line with all the rest of the things they were to talk about at that Conference, and it did not come from any one government — since four powers were involved, it must have come from the core of the four. They must have talked about something in reference to space because they also came out and announced the space platform. We give thanks for that to Professor Nahon, who in the first place, six months prior to that, introduced it into the Parliament of France through Mendès France and that's how it got to Geneva.[18]

You couldn't get better information from a higher authority than that. Now, all we have to do is settle down and have an open mind that the fears of others may not be promoted by your own fears — people fear what they do not understand. Once the fears go down, it won't be long before we can have the real truth about the whole thing, which is as real as you here sitting in those seats.

Here is a map of the planet Mars — all its lines etc. It reads on top "'Intelligent Life On Mars Possible', biologists say". Now it took several groups of scientists to come to this conclusion for one thing. Down the line it reads about the vegetation and things that have been discovered. This coming year they will have more

---

18 See also page 31.

information about this same thing, because last year they took 20,000 photographs from various parts of the world, from Africa to Pasadena or Palomar, and this was their conclusion. They say right here that at the junction where these lines meet, which are the canals, that it looks like cities are there. They have seen that much through telescopes and photographs which they took, through telescopes, so they are coming close to the statement made by Dr. Lowell[19] who was the first to promote the idea of life on Mars.[20]

Here's a diagram from Germany prior to the war ending. The Germans were already working on a flying saucer. It tells you all about it here — there are diagrams of all kinds. It was mostly propelled by jet propulsion, as you oan see. But, even then, we had started toward space and since then have moved a long way.

For those of you who have been wondering about contacts, here's something from Argentina. This is a drawing of a ship that landed there. If you would see that, there are four men marked in there in a transparent canopy, who, at the time of the landing were dressed in white. They were about 6 feet in height, The man who had this experience drew up one of these maps for the Argentine government and he sent me a duplicate. It is a map showing the territory — where other ships have landed in different parts of Argentina, also where they were sighted. If you could see my files, you would be surprised.

Another thing I want to make clear. I mentioned in my book about a metal — or slag — that I received from a ship under repair

---

19 Percival Lowell (1855-1916), an American businessman, author and astronomer, speculated that the lines which had been discovered on the surface of Mars might be canals.

20 Being at pains to emphasize that his contacts were with real people from the other planets in our system, as opposed to discarnate cosmic spirits that were increasingly being 'channelled' by mystics, Adamski used every astronomical discovery that might be seen as supporting his statements. However, according to Benjamin Creme, the life stream on Mars, for instance, moved out of the dense physical planes some three million years ago. Just as life on the other planets in our system it manifests there on the etheric physical planes, where Adamski's experiences took place. This makes Adamski's experiences no less real, or life on Mars any less physical, except it does not precipitate unto the dense physical planes of matter. See Creme (2010), *The Gathering of the Forces of Light – UFOs and their Spiritual Mission*, p.43. See also Appendix II. page 123.

on the second contact.[21] I do not I give an analysis in that book of what the metal was composed of, and you have a right to ask. Again, I could not publish it for a simple reason. When Desmond Leslie was here I gave him a bit of the metal to take to Great Britain to have analyzed. He did have it analyzed and this is the analysis, right here, from England. In the second line it says that the British government restricted it, and what they restrict, we restrict. Therefore, could not put it into the book, for if I had, they would have taken the book off the market. The reason the analysis is restricted is that two elements were found, according to this article, that are not known on this Earth. One thing is definite and proves in this analysis that the ships are made of aluminum and iron. The odd part is that as far as we know at the present time, *aluminum and iron cannot be mixed together*.[22] Yet it is done in this case and there is an important reason for this. Those of you who are scientifically-minded will agree with me — aluminum is a very good conductor of electricity, but it doesn't hold it. Iron does hold electricity, and these ships must have something that will hold the natural or static electricity as well as something that will give it off as fast as it takes it. We have proof now that the ships are made that way.

Questions and answers

Q. How do other planets handle weather conditions?
A. Nobody can handle weather conditions. If some of us knew how to handle weather conditions, we'd all want sunny days for our own personal needs and there would be no rain and the next thing we'd know we would have no food. Nature handles that. However, these people have learned to detect and control storms like we have just had along the coast of Florida. We have learned to do that,

Q. Did you actually visit the Moon as you stated in your book and if so tell us about the trip?

---

21 See Adamski (1955), *Inside the Space Ships*, pp.41-42.
22 See also Aartsen (2022), op cit, 'Exhibit #2, Physical evidence'.

A. I have. There's nothing much to tell, frankly speaking. Not much more than if you were to travel from Los Angeles to New York in a plane. You don't see anything when you are traveling in that way. You don't even know you are moving because there is no means of knowing how fast the ship is going by your reaction as you would in an automobile, or something like that. The only thing I can tell you is that space, itself, is dark even though the sun is shining brightly on our Earth. In space is much activity and it's not hot out there — it's plenty cold. When you get in a dark part of it, you'll see something like this: You know what a firefly is like when it is flying at night? (You have them here in the east). Well, it's as though billions of them, like snowflakes, moving through space, flickering here and there, but not producing light to illuminate space. Once in a while, you see a dark object, darker than space itself, that seems to be moving through space but you can't see what it is unless you look through instruments at it as it is moving. So that is about as much as you can see. Of course, when you get away from the Earth, the Earth begins to get smaller and smaller, and at the distance of the Moon, it looks much bigger than the Moon does when it is setting or rising, a lot bigger, and it has a very yellowish cast to it, not purely white.

Now as far as the Moon itself is concerned, and its craters — well, if you have a good telescope, you have probably seen movements and craters many times — even lights moving in the craters. That's been known by astronomers long ago. In fact, even in Galileo's time. But nobody seemed to know what caused the movement – one day there would be lights seen in the craters, the next day they were gone. Now it has come to be known that there are bases on the Moon that these people who are traveling our way use; the same as we are intending to establish bases on the Moon once we get out there. That has been the talk some time. While, on the other side of the Moon it is well populated and fairly cool. The side of the Moon that we see is about like our own desert. But aside from that, it is only a smaller planet and is chemically composed the same as our own. Some people insist it is a dead planet. You've never seen a dead form, living as the Moon has been living out there, al1 these thousands of years. It would disintegrate, had it been dead, by now.

But it is still there.[23] As far as the air around it is concerned, it has long ago been detected that there was air on the Moon — since a meteorite will not burn unless it encounters friction, and they have been seen to burn going towards the Moon.

Q. Will you give an explanation of Universal Law?
A. It is very hard to put into a brief statement. The universe is so big. But the briefest way I can explain it would be something like this: Nature is a law. It's a universal one. To go further, to give you some idea how the law of nature operates over forms, if you only want to look... The sun asks no question, what faith you may be, what color you are — or whether you are good, bad, or indifferent, according to the opinion of men. It shines upon you. That's a just law. It is not a respecter of persons or forms. That is the Universal Law, right there, in action.

Q. Have you come across any information about Mu or Atlantis in your contacts?
A. I have some information but not enough to talk about because the major job was to get this information that is now in the book and that's all. They didn't talk much about the past, but they do have records about this world dating back about twelve different civilizations. There was only one civilization of the twelve that did not annihilate itself. It was only slightly known on this Earth... It was the Triton race from which the Greeks borrow their Triton god, which is half fish and half man.

At this point, a minister rose from the audience and approached the speaker's platform.

Minister: Mr. Adamski, as Pilate said to Jesus as Jesus stood before him, "What is Truth?" We are all interested in Truth. The scientist

---

23 According to the Ageless Wisdom teaching the Moon as a heavenly Being (a planet) is indeed dead or dying. See e.g. Alice A. Bailey (1951), *Esoteric Astrology*, p.410. The liveliness that Adamski speaks of here, then, would refer solely to the bases that have been established there by the space people from other planets, and their activities.

speaks Truth. That's the reason I am here; to ask you a question. I don't wish to be petty or small but I am interested in finding the Truth. You have offered a challenge to religious leaders. I am an ordained minister of the gospel. I'd like to get down to the basic issues and ask you just a few questions. First of all, I have read your book. I am interested in directing a question concerning an idea presented in the book — the idea that is presented is that Jesus, the Christ, was a visitor from outer space, and that we have received other visitors.

Mr. Adamski: No — just a minute. We'll stop right there. Let's take one point at a time. It doesn't say that Jesus was a visitor from outer space. It does say there were Messiahs sent here and each time they have been killed, hurt, or something has been done to them, but it doesn't have any reference to Jesus, directly. It mentioned Messiahs, and if you took it that He was one of them, that would probably work in there.[24]

Minister: I don't have the direct quotation. I wish I did.
Mr. Adamski: I know what is in there, though. It could be confusing.

Minister: The idea was presented concerning that there have been many Messiahs.
Mr. Adamski: That's right. There have been.

Minister: That they come from outer space — and that Jesus was one of them.
Mr. Adamski: Well, let's go a little further. While we are talking about this outer space, we are not talking about a myth. We are talking about space that everybody knows exists within which planets are floating. This planet, itself, came out of space, it had to be born within space. So let's go from there.

Minister: The Bible teaches us that Jesus Christ was the Only

---

24 See Adamski (1955), op cit., p.182: "But even then we continued to send others out in the hope of aiding our brothers on Earth. These men were those known as 'messiahs', and their mission was to help their Earthly brothers to return to their original understanding."

Begotten Son of God.

Mr. Adamski: Very well. Let's stop there for a moment. If we go that far, who was the man who was known as Adam since he was the first man ever to step foot upon this Earth? Would he not also be the first man, the Son of God, of Whom he was created?

Minister: Adam, of course, was created of God.

Mr. Adamski: That's right. As an off-spring, he would be a son, as we understand the word son.

Minister: The scriptures do not speak of Adam as the Only Begotten Son of God.

Mr. Adamski: He was the only one on Earth according to that, but I sometimes wonder where one of his sons got his wife in the Land of Nod. Where did she come from?

Minister: But the distinct terminology of the Scripture is that Jesus is the ONLY Begotten Son of God, and the Bible plainly teaches us that Jesus Christ was unique, that He was Virgin Born. We might go so far as to say that the Scripture teaches us that He was God in the Flesh.

Mr. Adamski: All right. God in the Flesh, and for that He was nearly killed. Assuming that which He didn't assume but others have assumed. Just the same as a lot of us assume a lot of things. When He talked to the Pharisees and they wanted to stone Him to death, He said, "Why do you want to stone me — for the good works I have shown you?", and as He also stated, "As a man thinketh so is he". These men were thinking in terms of murder at that moment. And yet He went to their scripture, the scripture of the time, and He said, to defend Himself, "Know ye not that ye are Gods and the Scripture cannot be broken?" He called them Gods, too. All those fellows who were ready to murder Him; it's quite clear at that point.

Minister: Then are we to assume by what you have said that there is a plurality of Deity, because Jesus was God. Therefore these other beings that have come are Gods?

Mr. Adamski: Yes, let's stop there. If you read your Bible correctly, sir, you will find that statement to be true, because Jesus never considered 'God' as a Supreme Being. He considered God as a man. And in the Egyptian period when all the space ships were coming, since everything coming from the sky was supposed to be coming from heaven, when they saw them come down, they considered the visitors Lords, Gods, or Angels. But when Jesus talked about a Supreme Being, He said, "I of myself do nothing but the Father who worketh through me do all the works. I and the Father are one." And when He was on the cross, even at the last moment, He didn't say 'God'. He *complained* to God, by saying, "Lord, My God, why hast Thou forsaken me?," but in the same breath He also said, "I give my spirit unto the Father that it may return from whence it came." There's a difference.

Minister: Well, let's get right down to basic facts. We won't get anywhere, as long as we aren't going to agree on one basic point. Is, in your opinion, the Bible the inspired Word of Almighty God, the record of God appearing and moving, talking and revealing Himself to mankind?

Mr. Adamski: Since Jesus said to the Pharisees, "Know ye not that ye are Gods?" — yes ... for *all* men.

Minister: But in the sense that the Bible is the inspired Word of ONE God?

Mr. Adamski: *All* words of men are inspired whether he perverts them or not. Let me quote from this angle so that you may understand me. Since the first breath of life was breathed into Adam when he was created, that breath made him a living man, a living soul known as man. You show me yourself if you can live more than four minutes without the breath that you breathe and then if you can't, where you are getting your breath from. Is somebody dishing it out by the gallon to you, or is it free wherever you go and no questions asked? Where is it then coming from if it isn't coming from the Supreme Being of the Supreme Universe?

Minister: The first question I asked was if Adam was created by the Supreme Deity. You have answered that. Now, is it or is it not the Word of God — the Bible I am speaking of, the Old and New Testament?

Mr. Adamski: I grant you our Bible is all right. I'm not condemning the Bible. Don't misunderstand me. It is a very good history of man's growth in the things that have happened, and who governed the whole thing. It did put us in the relationship of the Supreme Being. At the same time, this is a universal thing at this moment that is happening. Don't forget that there are many other Bibles, too.[25] Many others that served a lot more people than merely Christendom. There are a lot more people who believe other angles than Christianity. Christianity is a small number in a sense. So we must acknowledge them all on the basis as a whole. These people are living too, and they are the creation of a Creator. (Applause)

Minister: I think that you misunderstand the main purpose of my question. In other words, I am asking not with the Bible as a history. I'm asking whether it is the product of the inspiration of Almighty God?

Mr. Adamski: All writings are a product of that since man must breathe before he can live and write. And his breath is holy if he understands it.

Minister: Everything of man is not of God.
Mr. Adamski: What is it of, then?

Minister: Jesus said, "You are not of God but of your father which is the Devil."

Mr. Adamski: He said *no* such thing! Paul said, copying after Jesus, "Marvel, marvel, for Satan himself shall become an angel." May I ask you a question, not that I want to put you on the spot, but to clear up some points. I don't like to put anybody on the spot. Is God – we'll take the word 'God' — all there is and outside of God is absolutely nothing? Is He all inclusive?

---

25 I.e. for instance the Indian Vedas, the Chinese Daodejing (or Tao Te Ching), the Arab Qur'an, and others.

Minister: No, how can He be?
Mr. Adamski: Well, brother. I don't know where you get it.

Minister: Is evil God?
Mr. Adamski: Isn't God all inclusive? Isn't God the totality of all that ever was in Eternity?

Minister: God is Eternal.
Mr. Adamski: All right. What is outside of Eternity? If God is Eternity then, we start from there.

Minister: Well, let's take the problem of Good and Evil.
Mr. Adamski: But where is it if Eternity is Eternity? What's outside of Eternity? Eternity is supposed to have no beginning and no ending and Evil must be within.

Minister: But God's creation is apart from Him.
Mr. Adamski: Now, if God is the only Creator there is, how come the Devil was created? Where did he get his creation from?

Minister: That is your question to answer. I affirmed it *as a reality*, sir.
Mr. Adamski: I'm taking your Devil. How was he created?

Minister: There is Evil. Shall we deny Evil?
Mr. Adamski: I know your point. I would like to talk with you on that — I could talk a long time on it with you in public or otherwise. But let me say this; Jesus said, "Have patience, for patience has a reward or recompense. For those who have lost patience become shipwrecks." Now, you mentioned other Messiahs that I wrote about in the book, as it was given me. Ch'in, after whom China was named, was a great Messiah to that race of people and he was asked what is Evil and he answered it this way: "Evil is an unripened fruit." Can we prove it? Yes. You yourself, as a child, no doubt picked an apple long before it was ready to be eaten — and if you ate a lot of them, you got a nice stomach ache. Your mother had to get a doctor. Very evil effect — all because you had not been patient enough to

wait until it was ripened. So, you might say the statement about both parties, or both Messiahs, one for the Chinese, one for us, are identical, in a sense — spoken at different times and conveyed in a different manner. I don't deny any of them — they all had their place. No one man constructs a building, it takes many talents to put up a mansion.

Let me tell you, sir, I have studied comparative religions, I've studied them all — I don't deny any of them. In the Catholic Church, you have the Father, the Son, and the Holy Ghost. If you see a picture, which you probably have seen, of the three sitting on a throne, you will find 24 cupids, little angels with wings on. You go to the Christian Bible and in Revelations you read in there, "Twenty-four Elders around the throne of God". You go to the Buddhist or to the Chinese, to their statue that represents Deity — naturally they are darker, they are going to color it after their skin, but still a human being — and it's got twelve arms on each side. Fundamentally they all speak the same language, represent the same thing — twenty-four Elders around the throne of God. Their arms are helpers, these cupids are helpers[26], twelve are in Heaven and twelve in the Earth. Yes, we can get confused, yet fundamentally they mean the same thing. You and I are not having any argument. You couldn't speak to me, I couldn't speak to you, if the breath was not granted to us by the same Supreme Being, whatever you may name Him.

Minister: I have the answer to my questions.
Mr. Adamski: Let me clear on another question that is brought up — on reincarnation. Reincarnation means to be reborn. Where in the Bible does it say you will not have to be reborn?[27] In our terms, it is resurrection, in other terms borrowed from the Hindu, since they are looking to the same God for help, it is called rebirth or reincarnation. So you see, labels are quite confusing, sometimes, yet fundamentally they mean the same thing. I don't deny your

---

26 The original transcript has 'helpless', which doesn't make sense here.
27 There is ample evidence that the New Testament evolved from a selection of early Christian texts, from which Jesus' teachings on reincarnation were removed when these were declared a 'heresy' by Emperor Justinian I (483-565), during the Second Council of Constantinople in 553 CE.

sincerity but if the religious bodies of this world do not open up and I mean all of them — I'll assure you that you will be alive to see it — every church that is open today might not be open in 1970, fifteen years from now. Because the generation that is coming up is space-minded, and they will follow science. We had better begin to blend if we are going to keep the moral standards. (Applause) If you could read my mail, you would come to the same conclusion.

Minister: You have presented Jesus in a light that makes Him *not* my Saviour, *not* the Son of God, that even Jesus, as such, represented Himself as the Word of God.

Mr. Adamski: Jesus *never* represented Himself as that. If anyone proclaimed Him for the Christ, it was Peter. He always claimed Himself as Jesus — read it correctly and you would not make that statement. Jesus always said, "I am in the world, but not of it". That is true, none of us are of it. Even the world is not of its own. It was not until when He returned from a journey which He was upon by Himself when He asked, "Who do people say that I am?" And the disciples answered and said He was Elijah, Moses, or someone else. He was quite discouraged with that kind of an answer so He said to His disciples, "Who doest thou say I am?" He handed over a key at that point – and that is when Peter said, "Thou art the Christ (he didn't say 'Jesus'), the Son of the Living God". Jesus confirmed it by saying these words: "Flesh and Blood (which was Jesus) hath not revealed it unto thee, but my Father which is in Heaven." Now as a result of this statement the Catholic Church accepted that and put Peter as the foundation of the Church as the man who holds the keys to the Kingdom of Heaven. Did you catch where the key was handed over by Jesus' statement? There's a lot more in that Bible than you probably realized.

Let us go over that again. I think it should be known to you for you can do much good. He said, "Flesh and Blood." Everybody judged Jesus from a physical angle as you and I judge each other. The physical angle does not tell us what makes that physical body tick. But Peter was so deep in concentration or meditation that he looked through that body into the body and saw the DWELLER in that body. And he called that the Christ. Jesus acknowledged it. When you and

I are able to see the Life, the Force, call it what you will, that actually brings forth every form regardless of whether it be man or tree or what it is that supports that form, makes that form possible, makes it live, then we are seeing, you might say, the Creator, face-to-face, in a small way. For no form manifests without this power. That's what that really means. That's when the key was handed over. Yet, we do find all kinds of groups studying the occult, the metaphysical, all sorts of things, and the key has never been realized by any of them. It takes more than a study, it also takes living. You must admit, sir, that had the teachings of Jesus as He taught them, let us say as just a man, (let's put Him that low for the sake of showing how great He was) been believed, they would have been lived. And had they been lived, we would have never seen the last two wars. (Applause) It's one thing to preach, it's another thing to live.

The Minister sat down and the questions resumed from the audience.

Q. Are there Visitors in the audience?
A. If there were I would not tell you.

Q. Why not?
A. For one reason, I don't betray a trust once it is placed in me. For your sake of seeing them, I would not place them in jeopardy if they were here. I am not a hypocrite and I am not a betrayer of human kindness. You are speaking from a selfish angle. Not only that, if you yourself were in the field of Real Self, you wouldn't ask me the question if they were here, you would know it. (Applause) I know when there is a strange condition about me, any time.

Q. Are they ghosts?
A. If you are looking for a ghost, they might be ghosts to you. To me they are as real as you are and you aren't much of a ghost. A lot of people have been trying to make ghosts out of them, that's true.

Q. They are not human like we are?
A. Then you are not human, either.

Q. What kind of communication did you have with the man from Venus?

A. The first communication was not much different than you would have a communication with an animal that you have not spoken to and he would understand you, like a dog wagging his tail long before you spoke a word. He would understand whether you are going to pet him or hurt him. Or not much different than if you had a mother 8,000 miles away from here and had not written to her for some time. All is well and then all of a sudden when you were the busiest, maybe, on that day you get a thought or worry what might have happened. It's the same method by which communication can be made, anywhere. That's the Universal Language, if you understand language. For instance, is there any human being here in the audience who has ever received a thought in a loud form as I speak now? All impressions and all motions of life are silent as far as promotion of the powers which are back of it. They go into action later. We receive a thought or an idea, then we speak in a form of words to convey it to another. So that is the true language of the Universe. However, the visitors do speak our languages. After all, they can tune in on our radios, if nothing else. But no life has been born any other way but through silence. No life manifests except only through silence and utterance is given after the impressions are placed upon that or any other form. Wen you study that a little bit yourself, you'll begin to find yourself, instead of a skeleton of a form that people recognize as a man. Then finally you will come to the point where you will be realizing when the Greek said, "Man, know thyself and ye shall know all things", you'll know the real thing of you, As it is now, your body and mine and everybody else's is nothing but a shadow, a casing in which that other power works, which is your Self.

Q. Do you believe cosmic power will be used in the future instead of atomic power?

A. That is very true. We are already hooking unto it and it's a matter of time now — we will have the first ship going on it. In fact, TWA[28]

---

28 Trans World Airlines was a major US airline that operated from 1930 until it was

has even got a contest in that field today. You can see what they're driving at in the year 1970.

Q. Did you feel any acceleration when you left the Mother Earth?
A. There is no acceleration because what they use is a force field. By harnessing the same force that operates our world, which we call atmosphere, around us. If you were at the fringe of our atmosphere, you'd know whether we are moving or not but being in a sea of the atmosphere, living right on Earth, like a fish in the water doesn't know the ocean is rough on top. They produce this force field, as it is known — something like if you threw a pebble in a still pool of water, you'll notice wavelet after wavelet going out until it reaches the shore. Where the pebble dropped is where the ship is, and wavelets like that are produced all around the ship; sometimes they are so strong they produce light and you do not see the ship at all when the force field is very heavy. They are actually flying within their own atmosphere, their own gravity, which they have built up according to the pressure of their own beings. When they come into our system or our atmosphere, then they blend.

Q. Do you have any information concerning the Geneva Conference?
A. I can't understand how people could have missed it. It was on the radio and everything — released in Geneva on July 16.

Q. How about psychic phenomena?
A. Psychic phenomena is a misinterpretation of natural phenomena. For instance, the words telepathy, clairvoyance, clairaudience, extrasensory perception and all those other labels are just labels. They don't mean anything different than what you were born with. All impressions come by channel of feeling[29] which comes through silence or by a form of silence unto you. Later you give it expression. And that's oftimes called psychic channel which is a perversion of the truth, in that sense. You are a material form materialized through birth from substance not seen before until it materialized into a

---

acquired by American Airlines in 2001.
29 Read: awareness.

form. The Earth is that very thing, itself. So we go into matter. We can prove chemically in a laboratory that matter is indestructible, while the form made up of matter can change from state to state, the true essence of matter is indestructible. So matter, therefore, is eternal. Therefore, if matter is eternal, the intelligence that governs matter and puts it into form from time to time is equally eternal. You don't need any religion for that understanding. It's scientifically proved already. There has been much confusion promoted because there has been much promotion on the materialization of the ships of these people which is a total falsity.

What a fool would I be if I could materialize and dematerialize as these ships are supposed to be doing, to buy a ticket in Los Angeles for New York, when I could, bingo! be there, deliver the message, bingo! be home and without any inconvenience. What a fool would they be, smart people like that to build ships of metals that are made of iron and aluminum, if they could do this. No, they still have to ride in mechanical devices the same as we do. They do not materialize or dematerialize in the sense that the idea has been promoted.[30]

One thing is definite, as far as your process of life is concerned, you couldn't die if you wanted to, if you understand it properly.

Q. Will you take a lie detector test?
A. I have said before I do not believe in lie detectors. They are no use in themselves. I begin to wonder how to classify your intelligence when you ask that. (Applause) I will say, however, I find all of you are very good sports. (Fin)

---

30   See also page 96, note 20; and Appendix II.

Appendices

Laura Mundo Marxer with George Adamski at dinner following his presentation in a downtown Detroit hotel on March 24, 1954
(Photo: Gene Duplantier)

APPENDIX I

Saucers! Simple as A.B.C.

by Laura Mundo Marxer, 1955

Each time I hear a new and more complex theory regarding flying saucers, and visitors from other planets, I realize how grateful I am to George Adamski for having made the visitors' coming such a simple, plausible thing for me.

When he came to Detroit to lecture on his experiences with the visitors in March of 1954 for the first time, I had the challenging job of handling the lecture promotion and consequently had a great deal of opportunity to listen to him as he spoke to the countless people who came to him, before and after the lecture. I worked closely with him during the other two lectures he has given in Detroit since then as well as handling his lectures in other cities. This has given me an invaluable opportunity to hear his story many times and to evaluate the information he has given out concerning the visitors.

From the beginning I recognized that George Adamski was far superior to me in conscious evolution and some sixth sense told me that if I was not concerned, as I noted that some people were, with any academic status or social graces, that he may or may not have had, I might learn something. And so I listened to *what* he was saying rather than *how* he was saying it and did not become personally offended because what he was saying did not always conform to my own present theories. I could see that those who decided that Mr. Adamski did not measure up, for one reason or another, to *their* idea of a man whom the visitors might choose to contact, lost sight of the message in their personal judgment of the messenger and they are the ones who have become confused. I sometimes wonder if perhaps Mr. Adamski was not chosen because of certain qualifications to give out this information to give us a chance to really see ourselves, regardless of what we profess to believe in. If any earth people are going to be chosen by the visitors to help to teach humanity a higher understanding of Universal Law, they would certainly have to prove that they could live the ones they already know, first, and that they are capable of growing with the new knowledge as it is presented and not limit mankind's growth to their own limitations.

Having identified myself with Mr. Adamski on the platform I found myself drawn into the field of saucer research and organizational work. Since that time, countless people have come to me for answers concerning the flying saucers and I am grateful that I have had the guide-stick of Mr. Adamski's explanation to give to them to compare to other theories. My own experiences with the visitors, just prior to Mr. Adamski's coming and many times since then have given me an opportunity to apply his guidance, to know that it is very practical.

Mr. Adamski lay emphasis on the fact that the people coming from other planets are *physical* people, of flesh and blood, body and soul, like ourselves. Because they *live* the Universal Laws as a way of life with every breath they breathe, rather than only professing to do so as many of us on this planet do, they have a more advanced civilization. They live and die and have children the same way we do. They are no closer to God than we are but have a further understanding of Him than we do and will help us to a further understanding of Him also, as they have tried to do many times in earth's history, if we will allow them to do so.

Mr. Adamski said the visitors told him that the combination of physical and spiritual like ourselves, body and soul, is in effect all the way up through infinitesimal schools of progress, back to the Original Source. It is *less* physical and *more* spiritual as we progress by being re-born on a higher planet of learning each time, providing we graduate from the curriculum prescribed in the school which we are presently attending. If we flunk, we take the course over. We are presently operating in the vehicle we built from our thoughts in our last life, in other words, our existence will be on a higher planet in the next life, since we are attracted to the vibrations to which we have progressed. We must raise our perspective from the old thought that sufficed when we had lesser understanding that "when I die, my soul will go to Heaven"... to the higher, more profound understanding of "when this present vehicle in which I am operating is defunct and has finished its purpose in helping me to learn the lessons I must learn, I shall graduate and be re-born on a higher planet of learning".

It is at this point that those who advance the theory that these visitors are Etheric Beings get off the track. They insist that the visitors exist beyond our seeing range on higher planes and only lower their vibrations and the vibration of their ships as a concession to our lack of understanding. They point out that Mr. Adamski has contradicted himself in saying that these are *not* Etheric Beings in his latest book, *Inside The Space Ships* on page 156 when he says that the visitors "can increase the frequency of the activated area of a ship to the point of producing invisibility". Mr. Adamski says in answer to that accusation that because a ship is vibrating at a too high frequency for us to see with our present range of seeing, even though it is hovering in one place in the air, does *not* change the essence or the nature of its matter. He points out that were one to poke his hand into the whirling blades of a fan that is moving too fast for one to distinguish the blades separately, one would soon know that the blades are still there and as solid as ever... and still very much within our dimension! If we were to think of these visitors as having further knowledge of *natural* or *physical* laws than we have, rather than get into any 'etheric' speculation, we might find it less confusing.

Since all in nature is gradual, it could be true that there are more highly perfected people whose physical vehicles are vibrating to a too high a rate for us to see and for even the visitors to see. These Greater People could be helping and guiding us from their particular fields of endeavor through mental processes and should they want to come down amongst us, they would have to conform to natural law and exist in a vehicle that was in keeping with our planetary rate of vibration, but *they are still physical people*, soul and body, and not spirits floating around. However, with these Greater People we are not concerned, especially, at this time. The visitors who are coming to us are within our vibratory range, with more refined atoms, to be sure, since they are more spiritually evolved, more in tune with the Universal Principle. As nature abhors a vacuum, she also does not jump from one octave to another, rather it is a blended, gradual process.

The fact that there could be other people like himself is the veil that man has pulled over his own eyes down through the hundreds of years. When the visitors came down through the past, he had no idea of the vastness of his *own* planet, let alone that there could be other worlds like his own and much more advanced. He obviously could not have conceived, either, of a 'flying machine' and its technical aspects, or he would have had one of his own. When he saw something flying through the air, it had to be a "living creature" ... like the birds, as Ezekiel described them in the Bible. He had no idea when he saw a strange "living creature" in his skies that people like himself could be travelling in it. Not knowing that people were inside this strange object, he did not connect the sudden appearance of an individual beside him, who might have emerged unnoticed by him from a ship when it landed somewhere nearby out of his sight. Discovering this person to be dressed in very superior clothing, showing a knowledge upon acquaintance far superior to his own, he at once thought of magic ... or the supernatural as we have come to call it. He connected these people with God, since he did have the ability to understand the existence of a Supreme Being in Heaven whom he worshipped. Anybody so superior to himself had to come from wherever God was.

It is strange that man should have developed a more mature, more profound understanding of almost everything else as his ability to conceive of more has developed, but still insists upon interpreting the incidents that happened to mankind through Biblical history from the perspective and level of understanding of the people of that time. Even though he *knows* that many times what seemed to be miraculous to the people in those times, is commonplace to us, and that even what seems miraculous to us today, we know has a natural explanation beyond our present understanding. He prefers to think it is blasphemous to consider anything in the Bible as having a natural explanation, forgetting entirely that behind the natural forces is a Divine Origin that no one is discounting. The religionist may talk about God but the scientist works with God's forces and certainly is not irreligious because he seeks to have a further understanding of them.

If he were to go back and read the Bible in the light of reality instead of childish fanciful myths, and think of those who came to help mankind in moments of emergency or to help raise his understanding at certain stages of his growth, or to start him on the right road when different civilizations began by giving him rules by which to conduct a society fitting for the understanding of the people of those times, we can easily see then that the God of Isaac and the God of Moses and the Angels of the Lord all could have been visitors doing the Creator's work of helping lesser evolved brothers to a greater understanding of Him. We, too, the visitors have told Mr. Adamski, will help to bring lesser evolved brothers on lesser evolved planets to a further understanding of the Creator when we have proved we can get along with ourselves and control our emotions and can once more be allowed to rejoin the Universal family from which we have so long separated ourselves. We have been given free will and choice to decide *when* we are going to learn the lessons both as individuals and as a planet of people, that we must learn.

We must push up the roof of our minds and *know* that all in nature is gradual, and that there are people more advanced than we are with degrees and degrees of growth between us and the Creator. However, these people coming to us do *not* want to be called gods as mankind has done in the past. They do *not* want to be worshipped, for they know they break a Universal Law that forbids *anything* or *anyone* being worshipped before God, Himself. In the past when they have come to help, man from his then present level of understanding, fell to worshipping them and they had to withdraw. They want to make sure that does not happen this time and so they are coming to individuals who can conceive of the reality of them and their rightful place in the Universe, who will, in turn, brief the minority concerning them. This minority, in turn, will also educate the masses concerning them to where they can come in and be received by all — a safe gradual method of growth.

Those of us in the saucer research field see in the Bible only a difference in the language of the writer in different times. The writer who wrote about Elijah's trip to Heaven in a fiery chariot wrote as best he could about a technical ship with non-technical language. A saucer researcher today would write that "Mr. Elijah was given a ride in a flying saucer" whose force-field about it lit up the ethers to where it looked like a ball of fire. He was given a ride to a planet to where there was a more perfected society, a comparative Heaven . . . *because the people lived God's Laws instead of professing to do so*!

We have been left alone for long periods of time to work out our own problems, the visitors have told Mr. Adamski, except for those who are constantly among us, guiding us. They are coming to us at this time for two purposes. They are watching our atomic experimentation very closely. They cannot come in and force us to use it for the good of all concerned, because they would break a Universal Law that has given us free will and choice to learn our lessons when we get ready to learn them. However, if we reach the point in our experimentation to where we endanger the planet and therefore the solar system of which they are a part, they can then come in and use emergency measures.

Also, they have noted a shift in the magnetic poles of our earth as would two bodies in conjunction with each other when one shifts. Our own scientists have noted the shift and the ensuing changes in climatic conditions that follows as a natural aftermath. The visitors have said that every planet has a slow third movement from north to south and that every many thousands of years, each planet takes a sudden quarter tilt and land that was under water comes up and land that was up goes down. It is only nature's way of replenishing a depleted earth after mankind has lived on it for centuries. They are watching this for their own sakes, for if the earth does take a sudden tilt, they would be prepared for the effect it would have upon their own planets and could move their people to a high place of safety which would be no trick for them, since their space ships carry hundreds of people at a time. They say that the atomic experimentation has not motivated the acceleration of our third movement but it can aggravate it. They say also that even with their own much more sensitive scientific instruments, they do not know when this tilt might take place, perhaps within the next few months... or not for the next hundreds of years. They make NO prophecies concerning this... or anything else, for there again they respect the Universal Law that says, "There shall be no other Gods before Me", which means the individual must learn to develop his own inner guidance, and anyone prophecying or giving him direct daily guidance is helping to break that law. The visitors, too, can only watch and be prepared and live each day as it comes along and will be glad to help us should we need help and IF we will allow them to do so.

It is *imperative* then that the work of indoctrinating the people of this planet into receiving the visitors proceed without interruption and those who are aware of the visitors and sit in meditation circles trying to contact them or attempting to bring themselves to a further awareness of Self only are pursuing selfish ends and spending energy and time that should be spent towards helping their fellow man to become aware of the visitors, for time is of the essence. Even if hundreds of years pass before the earth's shifting, those of us who are aware have a duty to mankind. There is no need to contact the visitors, they have said to Mr. Adamski. They know of each one of us and our efforts and are members of our saucer organizations, working right along with us. Those who seek for the visitors will someday be surprised to learn that they have been right at hand, all the time. They do not have time to reveal themselves to those whose only interest might prove to be the sensation of having had a contact, only to brag about it or to satisfy an ego-wish. After we have shown our good intentions of desiring to help make it possible for them to be received by everyone, as one would receive a visitor or a relative from a distant country without fear or undue fanaticism, they can then openly identify themselves to everyone and visit freely amongst us and once more extend a helping brotherly hand, should we need one.

Mr. Adamski has emphasized over and over, and made enemies doing so, that we *not* have any faith in psychic phenomena concerning the visitors... or we will be led astray in these "latter days". The visitors have said that wonderful intuitive powers will open up in mankind in general, eventually, and are opening up in some individuals in advance, as it always has but because our thought planes are only a reflection of the thoughts mankind has given birth to for millenniums, both good and bad, and some of them *very* bad, it is safer to stay away from such methods at the present time. With the physical plane being disturbed by the changes in the earth, the inner planes are equally disturbed and such methods as automatic writing, ouija board, trance mediumship and the new labels of the old psychic methods such as "voice precipitation on tape" and "omni-light communication" are all dangerous and can lead individuals down the garden path in time of an emergency. Also, invoking unknown universal powers as many groups are doing at this time, can lead to many dangers, the least of these being insanity.

The visitors have said that they receive our thoughts and are moving individuals who will allow themselves to be used into areas of activity where they can get saucer information to the people. They have a *plan* for coming to us, and are gradually indoctrinating people, consciously or unconsciously, to their methods. they send NO messages, however — moving people mostly under impression. If an individual does not respond to the impression, they do not force the issue, but withdraw and go on to the next individual. They give NO names — you will note that Mr. Adamski emphasized this in *Inside The Space Ships*. He said that the visitors gave him no names when he asked for them, but suggested he give them earth names if he wished for his own purposes of identification. Any information coming through any channel that does give this information can usually be traced to a psychic source.

Since all in nature is gradual, there are also people of *lesser* evolution than ourselves in the Universe, but still, also within our seeing range of vibrations. These are like intelligent children in their stage of conscious development and awareness . . . and because they live the Creator's Laws as best they understand them they are allowed to roam the Universe. They are *not* leprechauns and gnomes, etc., which is another strain of evolution by which God manifests Himself, with which we are not concerned either, but are the same strain of evolution as ourselves. They are scientifically in advance of us as Mr. Adamski has noted on page 86 of *Inside The Space Ships*, under the guidance of the Elder visitors, to differentiate between them. They are in our atmosphere and the Elders try to keep them back knowing we have enough of an adjustment to make to conceive of there being people like ourselves when we have been taught for so long that there could not be. However, they do get in and like children in trying to "help" sometimes create confusion. They do not realize the seriousness of the situation. They seldom make appearance because with *less* refined atoms than we have, they are more gross and not so "pretty". They have been the origin of the 'monster' stories. However, *they are not evil . . . that must be emphasized*, since in a well-ordered and controlled universe the 'evil' is quarantined as we are — and the non-'evil' allowed free pasture.

These Lesser People try to contact us, in any way that they can, even short wave radio, if encouraged to do so. Through a personal experience in September of 1954, I had a chance to see this explanation of Mr. Adamski's regarding the Lesser People, borne out. It is a long story in itself, but suffice it to say at this time that messages were beginning to come over short wave radio after a local group had attempted to contact the visitors. Because names were included in the messages and all kinds of advice and prophecies, I, myself, was able to evaluate them as coming from lesser people. Those who did not care to listen to my reminder of Mr. Adamski's explanations, found themselves running around the country night and day following useless directions in the messages, giving out prophecies to others that later did not come true and in general wasting precious time and energy. There is no doubt but that the visitors will use our methods of communication when we get them in here, since we are not so mentally developed as they are and must use physical instruments for communication. At the present time they are not using radio. Space has been such an unknown quantity to us that naturally we have not known this. I am glad I listened to Mr. Adamski for I was saved much heartache and headache in this respect.

The only safe method is to stay away from the sensational entirely and to be so busy working to help bring this information to our next door neighbour and relatives and friends that we do not have time to be tempted to try any methods, psychic or otherwise,

to contact the visitors. When the time is right for our own personal contact, it will reveal itself to us "like a thief in the night" and we will know in our hearts we will have earned it by helping to bring our fellow man a little bit nearer to his contact with the visitors and the wonderful heights to which they can help our civilization to grow.
The end.

(Source: James H. Wales, The Flying Saucer Information Center, Pasadena, Md, USA.)

APPENDIX II

The physical reality of the visitors from space

by Gerard Aartsen (adapted from previous publications)

According to the British Lord Brinsley le Poer Trench, the US Air Force test pilot who claimed he was present at Edwards Air Force Base when president Eisenhower went there to meet extraterrestrial visitors in February 1954 (see page 2), concluded his account of the event saying, "Then they displayed their para-normal powers and made themselves invisible. This caused the president some discomfort. The aliens then boarded their spaceships and left. All of us were sworn to secrecy."[1]

Other contactees, too, have testified to their contacts disappearing into thin air, such as Truman Bethurum[2] and the four young eyewitnesses to a UFO landing near Uitenhage in Eastern Cape, South Africa.[3]

Yet, in reply to the penultimate question — about psychic phenomena in relation to the appearance of space craft (page 110) — at the last of the three lectures compiled in this volume George Adamski says: "What a fool would I be if I could materialize and dematerialize as these ships are supposed to be doing, to buy a ticket in Los Angeles for New York, when I could, bingo! be there, deliver the message, bingo! be home and without any inconvenience. What a fool would they be, smart people like that to build ships of metals that are made of iron and aluminum, if they could do this. No, they still have to ride in mechanical devices the same as we do." Elsewhere he asked, "Why would a spook need a space ship?"

According to esotericist Benjamin Creme, in order to help us in all the various ways that they do, the Space Brothers need the

---

1 John Picton, 'Eisenhower Was Visited By UFO, British Lord Claims'. *Sunday Star*, October 24, 1982.
2 Truman Bethurum (1954), *Aboard a Flying Saucer*, pp.91-94.
3 Cynthia Hind (1982), *UFOs – African Encounters*, pp.138-145.

technology of their space ships. In fact, Creme says, "Many of the large ships (they can be up to four miles long) are mother ships, laboratories and so on."[4]

Indeed, when Adamski was on a Saturnian mothership, he was told: "This ship is a scientific laboratory. We travel space solely for the purpose of studying the constant changes within space itself. We observe the life and conditions on the many planets we encounter as we move through space. (...) It is through the research made by ships like ours that space travel has been developed to the present degree of safety."[5]

Italian contactee Giorgio Dibitonto, writing about his experiences in 1980, was informed: "The universe contains boundless regions beyond the material one that you know. The only dimension that is observed by your science is the material. (...) In the cosmos there is not only the material dimension. There are ultra-material dimensions that encompass not only length, breadth and depth, but a much greater richness of life-realities, as a consequence of which all of that which you call behind, in front of, over, under, within and without, become outmoded concepts. The higher a universe is, the more its life-force expresses itself in new, free forms, and the consciousness extends itself to a more comprehensive point of view."[6]

Contactee Howard Menger describes how he witnessed a flying saucer drop into our range of vision: "The ship took the form of a pulsating, fluorescent light, changing in colors from white to green to red. As it neared I prepared to take more pictures. It came in slowly, at about the speed of a Piper Cub. When it was within a foot of the ground and about a hundred feet from the car, it hovered, and I recognized the familiar bell shape. The pulsating colors stopped, it gave off an eery, bluish light, and then portholes appeared."[7]

However, as the majority of present-day humanity is fixated on

---

[4] Benjamin Creme (2001), *The Great Approach – New Light and Life for Humanity*, p.133.
[5] George Adamski (1955), *Inside the Space Ships*, p.135-36.
[6] Giorgio Dibitonto (1990), *Angels in Starships*, p.42
[7] Howard Menger (1959), *From Outer Space to You*, p.74.

the dense-physical aspect of reality, with little to no willingness on the part of the physical sciences to broaden their scope to include the subtler phases of physicality, and the subject of actual extraterrestrial craft fast being relegated to the fringes of scientific consideration, George Adamski's mission to inform humanity that we are being visited by beings from our neighbouring planets was always a tall order. Amid a rise in claims of contact by mystics, he was at pains to emphasize that his contacts were not space ghosts, discarnate entities, or imaginary 'galactic fleet commanders'.

A few months before *Flying Saucers Have Landed* was published, Adamski wrote to a correspondent about a follow-up book he planned to write, that "will clear this present state of confusion" and "even bring out a new and clearer phase of occult [= hidden] understanding which will blend perfectly with our present science . . ."[8] Note also this caveat in is his answer quoted above: "They do not materialize or dematerialize *in the sense that the idea has been promoted.*" (Emphasis added) Let us take this as a cue to take a closer look at the broader view of physical reality.

In the nineteenth century French physicist Jacques Fresnel proposed the existence of 'aether' as the invisible element that fills all space, which a theosophical writer explained as follows: "That which science postulates as ether is found by occult chemistry to be not a homogeneous body, but simply another state of matter; not itself a new kind of substance, but ordinary matter reduced [i.e. rarefied] to a particular state. We may have, for example, hydrogen in an etheric condition instead of as a gas . . ."[9] When experiments failed to prove Fresnel's theory, science abandoned the notion of 'ether' as a universal substance.

Before quantum mechanics gave us revolutionary insights into the nature of matter, Alice A. Bailey, a teacher in the wisdom tradition wrote that the atom "can be expressed in terms of force or energy. (. . .) The word 'substance' itself means that which 'stands under', or which lies back of things. All, therefore, we can predicate in connection with the ether of space is that it is the medium in

---
8   Adamski, Letter to John Williamson, June 17, 1953.
9   C.W. Leadbeater (1902), *Man Visible and Invisible*, p.8.

which energy or force functions ... Substance is the ether in one of its many grades, and is that which lies back of matter itself."[10]

It was the Swiss astronomer Fritz Zwicky who first proposed the concept of 'dark matter', which some scientists now see as a different kind of sub-atomic particle in a 'supersymmetrical' parallel universe "that behaves like an invisible mirror-image of ordinary matter."[11] Interestingly, Dr. Zwicky worked at the Palomar Observatory and is said to have visited Adamski three times at the Palomar Gardens Café, although he publicly ridiculed him.[12]

The Tibetan Master of Wisdom Djwhal Khul has said that the etheric "is the true form to which all physical bodies in every kingdom of nature conform" and that "life itself, the training to be given in the future, the conclusions of science and a new mode of civilisation will all increasingly be focussed on this unique substance".[13] When Mauro Raggi, researcher at the Sapienza University of Rome, in September 2018 said, "At the moment, we don't know what more than 90% of the universe is made of,"[14] there seems every reason to investigate if some or all of that could be this 'substance' or 'ether' that science has been unable to pinpoint in experiments.

Systems scientist Ervin Laszlo explains that the nineteenth century idea of 'ether' has now re-entered physics as the 'deep dimension' beyond spacetime, known as the 'implicate order', the 'akashic field' or the 'complex plane', which "appears to be a dimension or domain of the physical world beyond spacetime".[15]

In order to attempt a better understanding of the whereabouts

---

10 Alice A. Bailey (1922), *The Consciousness of the Atom*, pp.36-37.
11 Steve Connor, 'The galaxy collisions that shed light on unseen parallel Universe'. *The Independent*, 26 March 2015. See: <www.independent.co.uk/news/science/the-galaxy-collisions-that-shed-light-on-unseen-parallel-universe-10137164.html>.
12 Don Lago, 'Messages from Space'. *Michigan Quarterly Review*, Vol.54, No.1, Winter 2015. See: <hdl.handle.net/2027/spo.act2080.0054.108>.
13 Alice A. Bailey (1950), *Telepathy and the Etheric Vehicle*, p.139.
14 Ian Sample, 'Scientists hunt mysterious 'dark force' to explain hidden realm of the cosmos'. *The Guardian*, 3 September 2018. See: <www.theguardian.com/science/2018/sep/03/scientists-hunt-for-dark-force-to-discover-what-the-universe-is-made-of>.
15 Ervin Laszlo (2016), *What is Reality? The New Map of Cosmos and Consciousness*, pp.19-20.

of intelligent extraterrestrial life, let us expand our research with additional methods of questioning. As astrophysicists themselves admit they don't know where most of the universe may be found, we should remember that several discoveries which point towards more subtle planes of matter have so far been ignored, not only by mainstream science, but also by those who are looking for evidence of extraterrestrial visitors.

Based on his experiments British biologist Rupert Sheldrake says that dense physical forms may be seen as the precipitation of the 'blueprints' that exist on subtler levels, according to his theory of 'morphogenetic fields' — a sort of memory bank from which Nature retrieves its various solid physical forms.[16] Before Sheldrake, the Austrian doctor Wilhelm Reich experimented with what he called 'orgone radiation', first theorized by German biologist Kammerer as a primordial life force "which is neither heat, electricity, magnetism, kinetic energy (...) nor a combination of any or all of them, but an energy which specifically belongs only to those processes that we call 'life'. That does not mean that this energy is restricted to those natural bodies which we call 'living beings' . . ."[17] Like many trailblazers, Reich was persecuted, his books were burnt in 1956 and he was sent to prison in 1957 where he died that year. Interestingly, in the 1940s the Soviet inventor and researcher Semyon Kirlian had already developed a technology to photograph the energy fields surrounding living entities, which was later further developed to record human auras, now known as Kirlian photography.

As the famous theoretical physicist Werner Heisenberg said: "[T]he atoms or elementary particles themselves are not real; they form a world of potentialities or possibilities rather than one of things or facts."[18] Adamski himself already hinted at the solution to physics' conundrum when he wrote: "All Nature is etheric; whether in a form or formless state (...) when the word 'ether' is

---

16 Rupert Sheldrake (1981), *A New Science of Life – The Hypothesis of Formative Causation*.
17 Wilhelm Reich M.D. (1960), *Selected Writings*, p.195.
18 Werner Heisenberg (1958), *Physics and Philosophy: The Revolution in Modern Science*, p.186.

properly understood, you can see it has no reference to spirits or disembodied entities."[19] Elsewhere he put it thus: "The trouble with the metaphysical setup is that everything in the invisible is labelled 'spiritual' while in the visible it is labelled 'material', but in truth there is neither spiritual nor material — it is all the same..."[20] In other words, everything — physical or spiritual — exists at some point on the continuum of the same cosmic reality, from the three dimensions of our limited carbon-based reality to the dimensions beyond spacetime. Approached from a different angle, physicist and Nobel Prize winner Erwin Schrödinger confirmed the non-existence of a boundary between the objective (physical) and subjective (spiritual) universe when he said: "Subject and object are only one. The barrier between them cannot be said to have broken down... for this barrier does not exist."[21]

Thus far, the existence of phases of physicality above the dense, liquid and gaseous seems to be the only viable answer to the Fermi Paradox, which asks why we (i.e. mainstream science) have not found evidence of extraterrestrial life, despite the fact that it should be common in the Universe.

Given the intricacy of the issue, Adamski's one-time co-author and friend Desmond Leslie suggests: "Maybe his [Adamski's] mandate was to try and establish only the objective reality of the visitors; a difficult enough task in itself, without confusing the layman with anything remotely esoteric."[22]

---

19 Adamski (1957), *Cosmic Science* bulletin Part 1, Question 12.
20 Gerard Aartsen (ed.; 2022), *George Adamski — Letters to Emma Martinelli*, p.81.
21 Erwin Schrödinger (1958), *Mind and Matter*. As reprinted in Schrödinger, *What is Life*, combined 1967 ed., p.127.
22 Desmond Leslie and George Adamski (1970), *Flying Saucers Have Landed. Revised and Enlarged Edition*, p.259.

APPENDIX III

The Cross over Rome, November 1954

On several days in November 1954 UFOs were sighted over Rome, Italy. An eyewitness described the sighting of November 6 (see pages 7-8) as follows:

"At precisely midday I saw a perfect 'V' formation of twenty craft, the largest seen up to that moment, approaching from the easterly direction of Ostia. Almost simultaneously, I saw another identical one approaching from the 'opposite' direction. It was a matter of a few dozen seconds. The two squadrons met, joined at the vertices of the large 'V's and formed a perfect 'Andrew Cross' of exactly forty craft (ten in each arm).

The objects were flying in a V-shape or a diamond-shape and even an "enormous Saint Andrew's cross"

Photographic reconstruction of the event by the eyewitness.

"The cross rotated on itself by three-quarters of a turn, transforming into an X. Then the two squadrons separated, each forming a serpentine of 20 craft. After a few curves in the sky, the two serpentines disappeared from sight, rising to a higher altitude. The entire maneuver had lasted, in total, about three minutes."

Source: Sparviero 555 - testimonianza e articoli di stampa, December 12, 2011. <ufologando.freeforumzone.leonardo.it/discussione.aspx?idd=9915152&p=2&#last >.

Further reading

The Sea of Consciousness, feat. The Invisible Ocean
The Sea of Consciousness includes the integral text of George Adamski's lost debut *The Invisible Ocean*, two previously unpublished articles and a special clippings section documenting and demystifying his time with the Royal Order of Tibet. Plus three essays by Gerard Aartsen.
Paperback, 118 pages. ISBN: 978-90-9031695-6.

George Adamski – Letters to Emma Martinelli
Published in full for the first time, George Adamski's letters to his student Emma Martinelli, written between 1950 and 1952, shed light on this pivotal phase in his mission, and underscore the central thread of his teaching about the Oneness and universality of Life.
Paperback, 108 pages. ISBN: 978-90-830336-2-4.

The Adamski Book of UFO/UAP Disclosure
Recent confirmations from various disciplines corroborate fundamental aspects of George Adamski's accounts and teachings, including his photographs, physical evidence, ET contact, nuclear concerns, extraterrestrial life, consciousness, and the paradigm shift. With bonus material: *We Are Not Alone in the Universe*.
Large hardcover, 120 pages. ISBN: 978-90-830336-4-8.

George Adamski – The facts in context
A free website that documents the scope of Adamski's mission, the impact of his work, and the relevance of his teaching. Also features a unique illustrated biographical timeline.
Visit: www-the-adamski-case.nl.

www.bgapublications.nl

www.ingramcontent.com/pod-product-compliance
Lightning Source LLC
LaVergne TN
LVHW041849070526
838199LV00045BA/1511